FREE PARKS
FOR THE PEOPLE

FREE PARKS FOR THE PEOPLE

A History of Birmingham's Municipal Parks, 1844-1974

Carl Chinn

BREWIN BOOKS

First published by
Brewin Books Ltd, 56 Alcester Road,
Studley, Warwickshire B80 7LG in 2012
www.brewinbooks.com

ISBN: 978-1-85858-495-9

A Cataloguing in Publication Record
for this title is available from the British Library.

Typeset in Times
Printed in Great Britain by
Hobbs the Printers Ltd.

Contents

Acknowledgements

I would like to thank Councillor John Alden for first suggesting to me the idea of a book on Birmingham's parks. I had grown up knowing that parks, recreation grounds and playing fields were vital facilities for any municipality that aspired to provide the facilities essential for the welfare and wellbeing of its citizens; yet I had no inclination that the issue of free parks for the people was as significant as it was in the development of the Civic Gospel and the emergence of Birmingham as 'the best governed city in the world' in the late nineteenth century. Consequently I also thank Councillor Alden for setting me off on a trail of discovery that highlights not only the role played by philanthropists and councillors in the public parks movement but also that of working-class men striving for the best interests of their class.

I also thank Darren Share, Head of Parks, for his support, enthusiasm and expertise throughout this project; and I wish to acknowledge the vital help in sourcing photographs of Richard Albutt, formerly the Digital Programmes Manager at Birmingham Central Library, and Jim Hanrahan of Archives and Heritage, at Birmingham Central Library. Unless otherwise indicated all photographs in this book are courtesy of Birmingham Libraries.

Finally, an explanation about the period covered in this book. It starts in 1844 when Alderman J. H. Cutler first raised the subject of public parks on the Town Council; it ends in 1974 when Birmingham extended to take in the Royal Town of Sutton Coldfield because the subject of Sutton Park would necessitate and deserve a book in its own right.

Chapter 1

A Duty to Provide Recreation: the Campaign for Public Parks

It was a momentous day for the people of Birmingham when Adderley Park was opened on Saturday August 30, 1856. Covering ten acres and located just beyond the municipal borough boundaries in semi-rural Saltley, this was the first public park in the vicinity of the town. The gift of the local landowner, Charles Bowyer Adderley MP, it was welcomed joyously by the working-class especially. They craved a pleasant environment for recreation, living as they mostly did in densely packed and heavily polluted districts from which light, fresh air, sweet smells and greenery had been banished.

In just 30 years from 1821, as Birmingham's manufacturers had expanded massively to make it one of the world's greatest industrial centres, its population had increased rapidly and hugely by over 200% from 107,000 to 233,000. This remarkable rise was propelled by a high birth rate amongst local people and by migration of folk looking for work from the rural districts of the west midlands, mid-Wales, and the west of Ireland. The result was an excessive demand for housing.

This was filled by jerry builders who made a quick profit by hurriedly putting up thousands upon thousands of badly-built back-to-backs in dark and insanitary courtyards cheek by jowl with factories and workshops. To do so, they grabbed the gardens of the grand houses in Old Square and other central areas that had been abandoned by the wealthy in their flight to the suburbs, and they snatched whatever other plots they could find wherever they could.

The living conditions of the poor, in particular, were dire. In his major report of 1849 into the public health of Birmingham, Robert Rawlinson graphically laid out the severe difficulties that they faced. An engineer and sanitary reformer, he was one of the first inspectors appointed under the Public Health Act of 1848. He explained of the 220,000 people in the town over 50,000 lived in 'about 2000 close courts undrained, many unpaved and where privies exist they are a source of nuisance'. Of those he had inspected personally, large numbers had a:

> want of water, of drainage, and of proper pavement to the yards was common. Many of the courts are closed in on all sides, and are entered from the street by a common

passage; the privies and cesspools are crowded against the houses, and there is a deficiency of light and ventilation; there are about 336 butchers in the town, most of whom have private slaughter-houses crowded in amongst the cottages.

In his 'Report', Rawlinson made a number of recommendations relating to sanitary improvement. These included the provision of fresh water to each house, as well as the provision of drains, water closets and soil pans, paving, and street and court-yard cleansing. Interestingly in his thirteen-point summary of his Report, at number five he stated clearly that 'public parks and pleasure grounds would be very beneficial to the working-classes and their families'. Unhappily neither this nor his other thoughtful suggestions were acted upon. If they had been then the lives of scores upon scores of thousands of Brummies would have been improved for the better; as it was, for generations more the poor would continue to suffer considerably worse health and shorter lives than the middle-class.

A woman and a boy stand in a yard of dilapidated back-to-backs in Thomas Street in about 1882. These houses were soon to be cleared for the development of Corporation Street as part of the Birmingham Improvement scheme; they show the dreadful conditions highlighted 33 years before by Robert Rawlinson in his report that also emphasised the need for public parks in Birmingham.

Rawlinson was not the first person to assert the importance of parks, and not just in relation to Birmingham. Urbanisation and industrialisation were overwhelming huge swathes of the midlands, the north-west, Yorkshire and the north-east and in so doing were destroying open spaces. As early as 1833 a Select Committee on Public Walks had been set up to look at this problem, especially with regard to the loss of amenities for the working-class. One of its conclusions was that 'having a place to which they (the humbler classes) might resort on a Sunday Evening would tend to promote that self-respect which is so advantageous to all classes'. This factor would be one amongst a number that would soon motivate upper-class benefactors to give land for public parks. The others included concerns over public health; the reduction of disease as well as of crime and social unrest; and the provision of 'green lungs' for polluted towns.

In Birmingham, the subject of public parks was first raised on the Town Council five years before Rawlinson's 'Report'. In June 1844, Alderman J. H. Cutler had moved 'that inasmuch as there is not within this borough any public park or open space suitable and convenient for walking, amusement, and recreation, it is expedient, and would be a great public benefit and advantage to the health and comfort of the inhabitants, if a suitable place, or places, were provided for such purposes'.

Cutler's resolution was unanimously adopted, but there was a long way between support and action. The General Purposes Committee of the Council was instructed to communicate with the Lords Commissioners of Her Majesty's Treasury 'with a view to obtain a grant of money for providing public parks for the borough' – as funds had been set aside for this purpose. Unhappily nothing more happened officially despite the best efforts of Alderman Joseph Horatio Cutler.

He would seem to have been one of the many little gaffers locally. The prevalence of so many men and women who ran their own small-scale businesses in workshops distinguished Birmingham from many northern towns which tended to be dominated by a few large mill owners. According to the Post Office Directory of 1849, Cutler manufactured gilt plated pearl buttons, thimbles, hooks and eyes on New Town Row. As such he was one of the numerous toy makers of Birmingham, specialising in the production of small metal goods.

On October 5, 1844 Cutler wrote to the *'Birmingham Gazette'* in his personal capacity. The little gaffers were noted for their independence of thought and Cutler shared this characteristic. In his letter he pointed out that after the Council had applied for a grant, the Lords Commissioners of Her Majesty's Treasury had requested 'what amount the inhabitants themselves are prepared to subscribe, before they give an answer to the application'. Cutler deemed it the duty and the pleasure of all classes in both the borough and its neighbourhood to unite for this one object.

In support he quoted from a speech in August made by Lord Francis Egerton, MP for South Lancashire, at a meeting in Manchester to discuss public parks.

Egerton, a paternalistic Tory, had emphasised the debt that the rich had towards the working-class. He had asserted that public parks were no gift, rather they would 'meet a deficiency in my long account with the industry and energies of the working-classes of this town'.

Cutler declared that if all classes in and around Birmingham adopted such language then he could see a time not too distant when 'the inhabitants of this populous borough will have the opportunity of breathing the pure air, and enjoying those recreations so necessary to their existence, whether morally or physically considered'.

Two days after he wrote his letter, Cutler spoke at the Council meeting. He noted the request of the Lords Commissioner about fundraising locally and also their desire to be furnished with 'a detailed plan of the walks proposed'. Because the Council had not provided this information he felt its function in the matter had ceased and therefore he felt it his duty 'seeing the deep interest taken by the public in the question to place it altogether in the hands of the public'.

Within weeks, a public meeting was held at the Town Hall 'to consider the propriety of establishing Public Baths and the formation of Public Walks and other places of recreation for the inhabitants'. That Tuesday November 19, 1844 the Mayor, Thomas Phillips presided and 'amongst the company were many of the nobility, clergy, gentry, and influential inhabitants of the town and neighbourhood'. Amongst the speakers were Lords Calthorpe and Lyttelton, and the two Birmingham MPs, George Muntz and Richard Spooner. Alderman Cutler was also there. All of these men 'expatiated on the necessity of the establishment of the contemplated institutions, and the great and important sanitary benefits which must inevitably ensue to the labouring classes'.

More than £4,400 was subscribed in one week and a Committee was set up which thenceforth focused on providing public baths; but according to John Thackray Bunce in Volume 1 of *'The History of the Corporation'* (1878), 'the matter was, however, allowed to drop for a time'. Then in 1846 an Act of Parliament empowered councils to erect public baths and pay for them out of the Borough Fund. On October 7, this encouraged Alderman Cutler to move that the Council's Buildings Committee should be 'empowered to take the necessary steps for adopting the Public Baths Act' in Birmingham. It did so. By now the Public Baths Association in Birmingham had raised £6,000 and bought a site in Kent Street for 'their first experiment'. It soon transferred the land it had acquired to the Council.

Opened in 1851, the Kent Street Public Baths provided private baths for washing for men and woman and swimming baths for men – for a charge, of course. More baths were to follow but the issue of public parks seemed to have disappeared from the civic agenda. This was despite the fact that the 1848 Public Health Act had an associated enablement to provide funds to municipalities for the creation of public walks and parks.

The failure to take up this provision was one of many failures by the Town Council – but perhaps the most depressing of all was its inability to implement Rawlinson's recommendations. This inaction was caused by two factors: first, the division of authorities locally; and second, the antipathy of many property-owners to a rise in rates that would be necessary to pay for sanitary improvements. The Parliamentary Borough of Birmingham included the old parish as well as all of Edgbaston, and Deritend, Bordesley and Nechells from Aston.

Within this area the Town Council had but limited influence. Set up in 1838, it had to compete with seven other bodies: the Birmingham Commissioners of Street Acts, with powers of paving, lighting, cleaning, and regulating streets, and markets in the parish of Birmingham; the Deritend and Bordesley Commissioners, with similar powers; the Duddeston and Nechells Commissioners; the Guardians of the Poor of Birmingham; the Deritend Surveyors of Highways; the Bordesley Surveyors of Highways; and the Edgbaston Surveyors of Highways. This splitting up of local government functions weakened the Town Council and strengthened those ratepayers who vehemently and successfully opposed its efforts to implement Rawlinson's Report.

A year after its publication, the desperate living conditions of the poor of Birmingham were brought to a national audience by Charles Mackay, the special correspondent of the *'Morning Chronicle'*. Contributing in 1850 to a series on 'Labour and the Poor', he lamented that Birmingham 'suffers from the existence of about two thousand narrow, and for the most part undrained, courts which are the perpetual seats of typhus, and from the want of an adequate water supply'.

Mackay laid the blame for this harmful situation firmly at the lack of a competent central authority which could take public health under its control. According to Mackay, the absence of a firm and active authority meant that there was no sanitary staff in Birmingham who could compel the removal of nuisances, whilst there was no local control to stop either the overcrowding of back-to-backs or to compel the construction of sufficient drains.

Moreover, as the journalist bemoaned, 'those who consider public parks a necessity to every great town, will regret that, besides all the deficiencies above named, Birmingham does not possess a single acre of green grass where the public and their children can walk and amuse themselves'. Mackay noted that fifteen years previously, there had been a broad walk around St Philip's Churchyard. Standing on high ground in the centre of the town, it had been planted with large trees 'and although possibly not very salubrious on account of the encumbered position of the churchyard, it was, in default of a better place, the favourite resort of the people on the summer evenings, and of nursery maids and children during the day'.

Unhappily, the ground was too valuable as a burial place and the greater part of the trees were cut down, whilst the grand walk was dug up. This destruction of the

Greens Village in about 1880. This short street was soon to disappear for the cutting of John Bright Street, to the right, and for the extension of New Street Station. In his reports for the 'Morning Chronicle' in 1851 Charles Mackay revealed that in Myrtle Row, Greens Village, there was one water pump for 53 three-roomed back-to-back houses. This drew water from a well 'at the extremity of the row. Between 300 and 400 people lived in Myrtle Row and the water they pumped up was 'of a greenish colour, and smelling strongly of gas as if a gas-pipe had burst, and were emitting a stream through it'. A woman told the reporter that the water was filthy stuff and there was not enough of it to wash the house. For drinking she had to buy water at a ha'penny a can.

promenade angered local people so much that the workmen involved 'were obstructed and assaulted at their work, and constant riots and disturbances took place' until several men were arrested and imprisoned.

Mackay did point out that the Birmingham Botanical Gardens in Edgbaston opened their grounds each Monday to all comers for a charge of a penny. Still, at a time when every penny counted for the poor and hungry, there were many who could not afford even this small amount; whilst Mackay emphasised that as kindly meant as was this gesture, it did not supply the public want for 'the public require a park where they may stroll without payment – not only upon Monday but on every other day of the week'.

By contrast in London, St James's Park was 'both a botanical and an ornithological garden for the recreation and instruction of all classes at all times'; and it was free and open on a Sunday. So too were other parks in the capital and in 'every other civilized town and city' they also opened on Sundays. Yet in Birmingham the idea of opening the Botanical Gardens on that day 'was considered irreligious and subversive of all morality and decency'.

Mackay declared that two evils arose from this closure. Either:

> the working men of Birmingham and their families take longer and more expensive journeys in search of the fresh air and the green grass, the enjoyment of which is so essential to their morals as well as their physical health, or they pass the Sunday in the town in amusements that are by no means so innocent or so healthful, or pass their time in suburban tea-gardens amid gin and beer and

Bare-footed children in Hospital Street, Hockley in about 1906, highlighting the lack of space and greenery in the poorest parts of Birmingham well into the twentieth century.

tobacco-smoke, to the odour of which no female can be habitually subjected without the loss of self-respect and womanly feeling.

Finally, Mackay argued that the opening of the Botanical Gardens for a low price on a Monday encouraged some workers to stay off work for the day. Many in Birmingham were already well disposed to this practice of 'St Monday' and needed no further encouragement 'to waste a day that should be devoted to honest labour'.

Despite all these problems, Mackay recognised that 'the project of a park' had exercised the 'the anxious attention of many philanthropic men in public and private life' locally. Unfortunately the major obstacle they faced was the high value of land in 'the vicinity of such a thriving and expanding town'. This was made clear in August 1850 when the Mayor, Councillor William Lucy, was approached by Messrs Greenway, Greaves, and Whitehead, bankers of Warwick, who had bought the Aston Hall and Park Estate from the last inheritor of the Holte family.

The Mayor suggested to the Council 'the propriety of entering into a treaty for the purchase of the estate as a place of public recreation for the burgesses'. A committee was appointed but it was revealed that for 300 plus acres, a price of between £100,000 and £200,000 was sought. Whatever the exact amount it was a vast sum and beyond the resources of the borough itself, which was beset by a considerable debt because of the building of the prison at Winson Green and of other facilities.

A keen observer, Mackay was more than a critic. He put forward solutions for Birmingham's problems with providing a public park and drew attention to the admirable scheme in Birkenhead where a few public-spirited individuals 'have contrived to present to the fortunate dwellers in that town a public park, free for ever'. In fact, Joseph Paxton's Birkenhead Park is regarded as Britain's first publicly funded civic park but it was part of a residential development scheme that paid for the project. As such it was surrounded by attractive houses and wide tree-lined boulevards and its success inspired New York's Central Park.

Mackay posed the question whether the Birkenhead example might be imitated in Birmingham, so that 'by judiciously purchasing an eligible piece of ground of 200 or 300 acres, they may not lay out around it a belt for plots for ornamental villas for the rich inhabitants, and so make a third part of the park pay the expenses of the whole'. The question was well worth consideration both in Birmingham and other large towns lacking a public park within their limits for 'the health and amusement of the multitude of toiling men, without whose presence and exertions no town can be either great or prosperous and for whose moral and physical health it is the bounden duty as well as the interest of the governing classes, and the men of leisure and refreshment to provide'.

The urgings of Mackay did not fall upon stony ground – and it was not only the philanthropic rich who responded. On June 16, 1853, a meeting of working men was held at the Public Office in Moor Street. Birmingham did not then have a

Council House and this building served as a centre for local government, civic activities and public meetings. The purpose of this one was to consider the forming of a company to provide parks, gardens and recreation grounds for the working-class of the town. Representatives of leading factories were present.

They included those from the London Works of Fox and Henderson, the celebrated civil engineers of Smethwick who had supervised the building of the Crystal Palace for the Great Exhibition of 1851; from the Cambridge Street works of Winfield's, whose metallic bedsteads and gas fittings had excited comment at that event; and from Osler's of Broad Street, whose magnificent glass fountain had been proclaimed as one of the 'lions' of the whole exposition.

These men were joined by those from Elkington's of Newhall Street, whose electro-plated ware was varied and splendid; Wright's railway carriage works in Saltley; the Eagle Foundry and other establishments; and Laing and Company. This latter was a drapers, carpet factor and bedding manufacturer on High Street. It was distinctive in that it also employed women, whereas the other factories employed an overwhelmingly male workforce.

Importantly, letters of support were read out from Henry Wright, one of the proprietors of the Saltley railway carriage works; and James Taylor, the son of a wealthy button manufacturer. Taylor was a firm supporter of working-class self-improvement and had been the instigator of the freehold land society movement. When the 1832 Great Reform Act was passed, the qualification for voting was based upon property and the level was set at a level high enough to exclude the working-class.

However, two different types of franchise were introduced. In the boroughs, such as Birmingham, to gain the vote a man over 21 had to rent property valued at £10 for local rates. That was out of reach for working people, but in the shires the franchise could be gained if a man were a forty shilling freeholder. This meant that he had to own property worth £40 a year based on an annual return of 5%.

During that period, a decent house could be built for £70. Shire constituencies surrounding Birmingham included developing districts such as Saltley with its railway carriage makers. This qualification held out some hope for the best paid members of the skilled working-class. In order to gain property and the vote, they joined freehold land societies and building societies – both of which began in Birmingham. The freehold land society purchased a large estate in a shire at a wholesale price, divided it into plots and sold it on to building society members.

The representatives of the workers at this June meeting were the kind of men who could attain the vote. They pointed out that their employers had now agreed to the Saturday half holiday, whereby work finished at around dinner time. This shortening of the working week had long been sought and according to the *'Birmingham Gazette'*, the men 'were desirous of turning the advantage to the best account, and were now reasonably directing their thoughts to the best way in which they could spend their time'. They believed that this could be achieved by providing pleasure and recreation grounds.

These campaigning working men went on to draw an unfavourable comparison between Birmingham, 'with its scanty means of recreation for the working-classes', and places like Derby. Here the Arboretum had been gifted to the people by the textile manufacturer, Joseph Strutt. He had commissioned the highly-regarded John Claudius Loudon to create the new park and on September 17, 1840, when it was opened to the public, the whole town had taken the afternoon off work in celebration.

A leading garden landscaper, horticultural journalist and publisher, Loudon had also designed the Botanical Gardens in Edgbaston, which were opened on June 11, 1832. Three years later he wrote, *'Remarks on Laying out Public Gardens and Promenades'*. Interestingly his wife was Jane Wells Webb, who was raised at Kitwell Farm in Bartley Green. She was young when she was orphaned and perhaps influenced by her sorrow, she wrote 'a strange, wild novel, called *The Mummy*, in which I had laid the scene in the twenty-second century, and attempted to predict the state of improvement to which this country might possibly arrive'.

After her marriage to the much older and famous Loudon, Jane threw herself into the world of gardening. She grew roses and peonies with her husband and helped him with his experiments with plants. Soon she had become his secretary, copyist, researcher and note taker, and she played a key role in his massive work, *Encyclopaedia of Gardening* (1834). However, Jane was to make her own mark on

Birmingham's Botanical Gardens in the early twentieth century.

gardening enthusiasts. She claimed that books on the subject were too technical and so wrote *Instructions in Gardening for Ladies* (1840).

Clear and accessible and including personal sketches of and stories about gardeners, it pushed forward gardening as something suitable for ladies and sold more than 20,000 copies. She followed this with *The Ladies Flower Garden* (1843-44) and other books. Unhappily, the talents of the Loudons were not used more in Birmingham with regard to the provision of public parks.

The working men at the June meeting in 1853 also compared Birmingham adversely with Manchester. It too, had gained a charter of incorporation in 1838, but since then its Council's proactive approach had shamed slothful Birmingham. In 1844, Manchester had banned the building of back-to-backs whilst Birmingham was not to do so until 1876; and this swift response to the massive problem of bad housing was matched by that towards the provision of public parks. The main campaigner for these was Mark Philips, MP for Manchester. In May 1843, he pronounced that the town needed to make provision for 'some public walks or places of recreation for our over-worked and under-fed population'.

A fund was begun and a year later the Government gave it £3,000, whilst private donors provided a further £30,000. These efforts led Manchester Council to set up a Committee for Public Walks, Gardens and Playgrounds in 1845 and the next year the authority opened its first three public parks: Queen's Park and Philips Park in Manchester, and Peel Park in adjoining Salford. These were the first public parks in a large town outside London. Although paid for by public subscription, they were owned by the Council and in 1856 Manchester would go on to appoint John Shaw as the first Inspector of Public Parks for the borough.

By then, Manchester boasted Owens College, the precursor of the modern Manchester University and it had become the first large town to open a free library under the Free Libraries Act of 1850. Birmingham was again behind the times. In March 1852 the Council resolved that that the Mayor, Henry Hawkes, should take the necessary steps to determine whether or not the Public Libraries Act should be adopted. This legislation required that a poll had to be taken of the ratepayers and that two-thirds needed to be in favour for the Act to be adopted.

The adoption was opposed virulently by those many ratepayers who wished to avoid an increase in the rates for the building and stocking of libraries. They were supported by those who opposed the expansion of local and national government. In his *'Old and New Birmingham'* (1880), Robert K. Dent denounced them all as lovers of 'darkness and ignorance'. Polling took place on April 7, but although the supporters of adopting the Act won by 534 to 363 they did not have the required two-thirds majority. With justification, Dent bemoaned the fact that 'the intellectual advancement of the people was retarded for almost a whole decade'. Indeed the Act was not adopted until 1860.

Birmingham did not merely lag behind Manchester – it was not even in the race to provide facilities for the education and recreation of its citizens; too few of its leading citizens cared. This inertia could have been excused as having been the result of the division of powers locally. However in 1852, the Council finally became the sole local authority when it took over the roles of the Street Commissioners and similar bodies covering Deritend and Bordesley. There was now an opportunity to for the Council to become proactive, but the hopes of those who yearned for dynamic leadership were dashed.

The dominant ideology amongst councillors remained one of economy, parsimony and inaction. Men such as Alderman Cutler who wished to see the Council act positively were a rare breed. According to the eminent historian, Asa Briggs, in the 1850s the Council was 'lacking in both dignity and vision'. It refused to appoint a medical officer of health, where Liverpool had done so in 1847; and expenditure on public works such as drainage and sewerage was reduced considerably.

In such a negative setting, the optimism of the working men in campaigning for public parks at their meeting in 1853 was remarkable and praiseworthy. They affirmed that it was 'an evil to have so many thousand people working daily in such an unhealthy atmosphere of that of Birmingham, without grounds for recreation which they could call their own, and to which they could have access whenever they required relaxation'. Accordingly they resolved 'that grounds for public recreation were desirable, and might be purchased by the cooperation of the working-classes'.

Towards the end of the meeting, Joseph Sturge spoke briefly. A wealthy corn merchant who lived in Edgbaston, he was a devout Quaker and abided by the belief that every hour of each day a Christian had to do the will of Jesus, the prince of peace. When revolutions convulsed Europe in 1848, he went to their focal point in Paris and attended a peace congress; when famine ravaged Ireland and Finland he endeavoured mightily to bring aid to the starving; when destitute youths in Birmingham had no hope he founded a home for them; and when working-class teenagers and young men locally needed an adult school he encouraged Quaker friends to start one.

In the same ways, wherever there was injustice so did Sturge strive to overcome it. He abhorred slavery and after its supposed abolition in British colonies in 1833, he visited the West Indies and worked tirelessly for the wellbeing of freed slaves. Jamaicans, especially, remembered him for 'his long, arduous and unwavering advocacy of their rights as men and British subjects'. He was as devoted an advocate for the rights of the working-class in England, believing ardently that working-class men should have the vote and not be excluded from the political nation through class prejudice.

In his short address at the 1853 meeting discussing the desirability of public parks locally, Sturge recommended that the workers did not 'rely too much on their own pecuniary means but endeavour to obtain all the aid that they could from those above them in society'. In particular he felt that an appeal could be made to the large landowners of the town 'some of whom he had no doubt would willingly grant a few acres of land for the purpose of public recreation, and that too upon higher considerations that it would greatly improve the value of the surrounding property'.

The working-men's meeting elected a provisional committee to carry out the resolution to form a company to provide parks, gardens and recreation grounds for the working-class of the town. This gathering of the representatives of the working-class was well-publicised in the *'Birmingham Gazette'*, a Tory newspaper, and it seems it had had a swift and positive outcome in stirring some leading citizens into doing something. Just a few weeks later, on July 26, 1853, 'an influential preliminary meeting' was held at the Public Office 'to take into consideration a project providing a public park for the inhabitants of the town'.

It was presided over by the Mayor, Henry Hawkes. An attorney, he was a vigorous supporter of political and social reform and in the 1840s had formed a Working Man's Society to build a People's Hall in Loveday Street. Hawkes was elected to the Council in 1846 and came to be admired as 'the ablest member of that body'. Praised in *'Faces and Places'* in 1889 as 'a clear and incisive speaker, a close reasoner, a ready and finished debater', he was broad-minded and democratic of spirit. As such Hawkes was the antithesis of the small-minded and mean-spirited Economists who unfortunately dominated the Council.

He was joined at the meeting by others of a reforming desire. They included Joseph Sturge; George Muntz, one of the two MPs for Birmingham; Robert L. Chance, the enlightened glass manufacturer of Smethwick; Henry van Wart, an American merchant who was the brother-in-law of the father of American literature, Washington Irving; and George Edmonds. A longstanding radical in politics, Edmonds had been imprisoned in 1821 for his beliefs in parliamentary reform and was praised ten years later for his devotion 'to the great cause of public liberty, and more especially to the rights, privileges, and welfare of his fellow-townsmen'.

The first to speak at the meeting was Samuel Beale, a former Mayor and a leading businessman. He had been instrumental in founding the Birmingham and Midland Bank in 1836 and was a director of the Midland Railway. Beale explained that he had recently met an influential man from Sutton who mentioned that the townsfolk were bent upon having a railway. Beale suggested that the Midland Railway could do this via a branch line from Bromford. He then outlined his thoughts that the Sutton Corporation should provide Birmingham with 250 acres of Sutton Park for 999 years at a pepper-corn rent of one shilling an acre; whilst Birmingham would erect a grand structure like the Crystal Palace at a cost of from £20,000 to £30,000 – and next to which the Midland Railway would open a station.

Such a scheme would provide an income for the railway via visitors to the park, which would be open to Suttonians as well as Brummies; and it would require but

A wonderful photograph dating probably from the mid-1890s. In the background from left to right are the clock tower of the Museum and Art Gallery; the dome of the Council House; and the spire of Christchurch, which was knocked down in 1898. To the right is the Old Wharf canal basin, whilst to the left the building in the foreground had been Cadbury's factory before it was moved to Bournville. The buildings behind had been part of the Eagle Foundry, some of whose workers attended the meeting of working men on June 16, 1853 to press for parks. The headquarters of the Birmingham Municipal Bank and Register Office were later built on this site. Today the Register Office is the House of Sport.

a small increase in the rates to pay for the building. In that period rates were paid only by property owners and in supporting the idea, Muntz made it plain that the more prosperous owed a moral duty to those who laboured for them, and to whom they owed all they possessed. Indeed he proclaimed, 'was it not a duty to provide for those whose means of recreation had been banished from the town?'

The meeting was also attended by a Mr Simpson, the chairman of the Artisans' Half-Holiday Movement. On behalf of his committee and the 20,000 artisans who belonged to the movement, he promised 'that the scheme would be hailed with gratitude and pleasure by the working men'. A deputation was agreed upon to discuss the proposals with the Corporation of Sutton Coldfield. Unsurprisingly, given the vague nature both of Beale's discussion and the difficulty of bringing all the parties together let alone to agreement, the idea fell by the wayside.

Though it had failed, still did it succeed in maintaining public interest in the public parks movement. A few months later, on December 22, 1853, the Mayor, Mr James Baldwin, called a meeting of the ratepayers 'to consider the propriety of authorising the Town Council to make application to Parliament for power to enable the Council to accept grants of, and to purchase, lands to be used as places of recreation'.

Baldwin was another dedicated reformer. He had started out as a working man but went on to become the owner of Sherbourne Mill, Kings Norton where his firm also made paper and paper bags. In particular, Baldwin was a prominent figure locally in the campaign against the 'taxes on knowledge'. These were the Stamp Acts which required the payment of a stamp on each single newspaper and pamphlets. Obviously, this law caused a drastic increase in the cost of such printed material, badly affecting not only the spread of democratic views but also the economic viability of the printing trade. After a vigorous campaign the stamp was reduced to one penny in 1836 and the measure was abolished in 1855.

Joseph Sturge was again in attendance at this December meeting, as was Birmingham's other MP, William Scholefield; so too was Charles Bowyer Adderley. He and Lord Calthorpe had both made offers of land for parks but the Council felt it needed an act of Parliament to avail itself of these offers. Moreover, as the Mayor emphasised, such a measure 'would doubtless be the means of encouraging other landowners to follow their example, as the object of the Council was not the establishment of one large park but the formation of several in various quarters of the town so that the inhabitants might be within easy access of some one of them'.

The Mayor then asked the Town Clerk, Mr Morgan, to speak. He explained that the Borough Improvement Act of 1851, which had transferred local government entirely to the Town Council, had also devolved certain obligations. These included 'the promotion of healthy and rational enjoyment, the kindly intercourse, and good morals of the community'. In support of public parks, Scholefield observed that the Council and other bodies had expended great sums in building 'gaols, workhouses and lunatic asylums, and it was perhaps not too much to say that many of the occupants of these places had been driven to intemperance and excesses for want of rational amusement and places of recreation'.

This issue of rational recreation was of pressing importance to middle-class reformers. They feared and abhorred the rough amusements of many working-class men. Blood sports such as bear and bull baiting were not only cruel but they brought together large numbers of rowdy men who threatened public order. Evangelical Christians particularly strove to eliminate what they regarded as bloody, immoral and potentially riotous pastimes. Their assault on traditional leisure activities was strengthened by the efforts of factory owners who were seeking to impose a time and work discipline on their employees.

Big units of production and big machines were expensive and employers could not afford to have them idle if large numbers of men took Mondays off. Factory owners sought to ensure regular attendance by fines from wages and by supporting moves against popular amusements. Thus whilst national legislation banned blood sports, local opposition ended long-established wakes and fairs which encouraged people to take time off from work. Such events also needed large spaces and these were disappearing under the urban onslaught.

Yet if the middle-class were determined to reform working-class leisure activities, so too were many working-class men and women – but for different motives. They disliked gambling and heavy drinking because they strained inadequate incomes and diverted men away from political agitation; whilst they shunned rough sports because of their own beliefs and concepts of morality – whether they were Christian or not. Such activities, then, were decried as not worthy of respectable working men. These beliefs were strongest amongst artisans, skilled men who were regularly employed and who enjoyed better incomes than the semi-skilled and unskilled. And in Birmingham it was they who were pressing for public parks as somewhere where working-class people could pass the time healthily, morally and rationally.

A few employers shared their feelings. Joseph Sturge, especially, was one of those few employers who acted caringly for others and whose actions were not motivated by profit and the desire to control the working-class. At the December 1853 meeting he regretted that 'there was not a town in England so ill-provided with playgrounds as Birmingham. The children could not enter a field without trespassing, and it was a serious injury to their health to be deprived of the means of recreation'.

Sturge stated that he had been told by his friend and fellow Quaker, Richard Cadbury, that in 1800 when the town had only 80,000 people they had the benefit of 5,000 gardens in and about the town, 'so that there was hardly a poor family that had not a bit of ground'. Now these had been destroyed 'so that the children of the poor had scarcely a back door to go out of, or a yard of ground to play upon'.

The gardens to which Cadbury referred had been known as 'guinea gardens'. In the first *'History of Birmingham'* in 1787, William Hutton explained that 'a small part of the land near the town is parcelled out into little gardens, at ten or twenty shillings each, amounting to about sixteen pounds per acre'. They were intended not 'so much for profit, as health and amusement'. By the early nineteenth century, the usual rent for a good-sized garden of 300 square yards was a guinea (£1.05) a year, hence their name, and their number had increased significantly.

In 1825, James Drake in his *'Picture of Birmingham'* observed that from the canal-side off Broad Street, now Brindley Place, walkers could:

> enjoy a pleasing and lively summer-view over a considerable tract of land, laid out in small gardens. This mode of applying plots of ground, in the immediate

> vicinity of the town, is highly beneficial to the inhabitants. There must be some thousands of these gardens in different quarters round Birmingham, letting from 10s 6d to two guineas per annum.
>
> They promote healthful exercise and rational enjoyment among the families of the artizans and with good management, produce an ample supply of those wholesome vegetable stores, which are comparatively seldom tasted by the middling classes, when they have to be purchased.

Drake added that such gardens had formed a feature 'almost peculiar to Birmingham; but latterly this profitable adaptation of ground has been practised near many other towns'. In fact by the mid-1820s, the guinea gardens had surrounded most of the town. In the east, they covered much of Bordesley, Ashted and Duddeston; in the north, most of Hockley and Summer Lane; in the north-west, the greater part of the Jewellery Quarter; to the west large swathes of Ladywood; to the south west, nearly all of Lee Bank; and to the south east, parts of Deritend and Highgate.

These guinea gardens were of a good size and in his *'Century of Birmingham Life'*, John Alfred Langford noted that they were a 'hobby with the Birmingham working-man, and the cultivation of flowers was carried to great perfection by him. Summer evenings and Sunday mornings were the usual times of labour in this his modern paradise; and on Sunday afternoons and evenings he used to take his wife and family to rejoice in his floral treasures'.

Some gardens were also used for growing vegetables, and others that were even more expansive gave opportunities for play and walking. An advertisement in the *'Birmingham Gazette'* for July 1815 offered a three guinea garden for sale by auction. This was big enough to abound 'with numerous choice young Fruit Trees of superior Sorts, Flowering Shrubs, and Vegetables, a capital Wood Summer House, and a Pump of Soft Water; the whole judiciously displayed, situate and being the third Garden on the Left Hand side of the first Walk on the Right of Summer Lane'. This garden was very close to the General Hospital, which did not move to Steelhouse Lane until the end of the nineteenth century.

For all the middle-class fears of rowdy and rough working-class amusements, many of Birmingham's working-class men had long enjoyed healthy and rational recreation. It had not been imposed upon them; it was inherent to them, their lives and their values. And it was the loss of these guinea gardens that pushed many artisans into campaigning for public parks. Sturge was both alert to their loss and sympathetic to their cause and at the December meeting he stated that he had a piece of land at Edgbaston which he leased for £50 a year. If the Town Council were to accept it then he would be happy to give it up.

Sturge's importance to the movement for public parks was emphasised by the next speaker, Charles Bowyer Adderley MP. He was an intriguing character. Later the first Baron Norton of Norton-in-the-Moors Staffordshire, his county seat was Hams Hall, near Whitacre in Warwickshire and he was the lord of the manor of Saltley, owning the chief estates both there and in Washwood Heath. A Tory, leading Anglican and wealthy landowner, Adderley appeared the epitome of the privileged upper-class – yet he was deeply committed to practical social projects that improved the lives of the working-class and of those living in British colonies.

As a key government figure, he promoted colonial self-government in New Zealand and Canada, and he successfully campaigned against the transportation of criminals to Cape Town. There he is recalled in an Adderley Street, as he is in Birmingham. Adderley also believed passionately in the positive force of education and pushed for the foundation in 1850 of the Saltley Church Training College, afterwards called Saint Peter's College for the training of teachers. Five years later, he proposed the reformatory schools bill and his enlightened belief that education was a more effective deterrent to crime than punishment led him to found the Saltley Reformatory, better known as the Norton Boys Home.

In his address to the December 1853 meeting, Adderley proclaimed that he was there 'as a Birmingham man to take part with them as Birmingham men in carrying out a measure of great social improvement'. He realised that there were not as many people in attendance as at previous meetings that had discussed the issue of public parks, but he believed that the smallness of the meeting proved its necessity.

It showed 'very clearly that the working-classes were closely confined at labour; that they had not time to attend a meeting of such importance to themselves, and that they stood in great need of grounds of recreation and amusement after the toils and labour of the day were over, or at such other times as they could spare for relaxation'. Adderley was certain that irrespective of party, politics and religion, everyone was supportive of the public parks movement because 'all were alike interested in the promotion of healthful and rational enjoyments'.

Adderley could envisage no opposition and he looked fondly to a time when in Birmingham 'the peer and the peasant, the master and his men, the shopkeeper and his assistants – in fact, when all classes would be seen together, enjoying themselves in those manly sports and amusements which once were the pride and happiness of the people'. Cricket, of course, was such a sport and with the lack of space in large towns, its playing was impossible.

If Adderley's vision was utopian, then his sentiments were worthy. Once again, Henry Wright of the Saltley railway carriage works expressed his support. In a letter read out by the Town Clerk, he suggested that 'the manufacturers of Birmingham who derived advantage from the labour of the industrious classes ought to provide for their recreation'.

Amongst the other speakers was George Dawson, one of the most charismatic and influential figures in the history of Birmingham. A preacher and pastor born in

London, he had come to Birmingham in 1844 aged just 23 to take charge of the Mount Zion chapel. Markedly independent of mind, Dawson soon moved on to his own Church of the Saviour in in Edward Street, later the 'Lyric' picture house. Here worshippers of all faiths were pulled in by the appeal of this extraordinary man.

Of middle height, robust and broad set, Dawson's black hair cascaded down over his ears and his forehead, and a thick beard flowed over his neck and to the top of his chest. Dressed in a long velvet coat that stretched to his knees and a colourful necktie, he was one of the most powerful speakers of the age. He declared that Jesus had not died for man but lived for him, and he exhorted his listeners to follow Our Lord's example and not think of what should not be done but of what more could be done.

Dawson chastised those who did not live their beliefs daily and who felt that they need only act as Christians on a Sunday. He urged each citizen to strive 'to clothe the naked, to feed the hungry, and to instruct the ignorant'. And he proclaimed that 'a great town is a solemn organism through which should flow, and in which should be shaped, all the highest, loftiest and truest ends of man's intellectual and moral nature'.

In the 1870s, Dawson's preaching and passion would deeply affect Joseph Chamberlain and others to act on this Civic Gospel and to transform Birmingham into 'the best-governed city in the world'. Now, though, in the Birmingham of the early 1850s that was dominated by lacklustre councillors, he was struggling to push

The 'Lyric' picture house in Edward Street in the 1950s; it was formerly the Church of the Saviour, where George Dawson preached.

forward his radical message of social reform through political action. Despite this, he remained outspoken – and outspoken he was at the December meeting.

He urged the Mayor to get rid of the 'priggish mode' of calling the town's meetings at 12 noon 'when the people could not attend. The working men had to earn their dinner and then to eat it, and they could not attend a meeting at the same time'. To this end he hoped that in future meetings would be called when the people could and would be there – in the evening. Dawson then expressed his support for a public park for 'it was a good object, a most desirable one, a most necessary one'.

He always paid his rates cheerfully when he knew they were for a proper object and 'right heartily would he pay the penny rate which was to provide play-ground for the children and working men and women of the town'. In fact he would 'rather have one good park than ten museums'. Both were good and useful but 'the grounds for recreation should always have the preference'.

Soon after Dawson spoke the Mayor put the resolution to the meeting that the assent of the ratepayers should be sought to authorise the Town Council to apply to Parliament 'for power to enable the Council to accept grants of, and to purchase, lands to be used as places of recreation'. It was carried unanimously and the ratepayers went on to adopt it. The next year, 1854, an 'Act for establishing Parks in or near to the Borough of Birmingham' was passed.

This empowered the Council 'to accept any gifts, grants, or devises of land' for such a purpose, 'and to provide for the maintenance of the same as public places of recreation, to levy a rate of one penny in the pound for such purposes, and to borrow at interest on the security of the borough rates, or of the separate rate authorized by this act, any sum not exceeding £30,000'.

Unhappily, the pugnacious and often abusive Joseph Allday now dominated the Council. If before that body had been written off as uninspiring, under his leadership from 1854 it seemed to revel in retrenchment. Cost-cutting was Allday's only motivation and reduced rates his only objective. The provision of a public park would add to the rates, and that fact doomed any thought of the Council providing one or even supporting the provision of one.

That was made plain in 1855 when Adderley offered the Council ten acres of his land at Saltley for a public park. His conditions for such liberality seemed undemanding. He asked that the Council should pay a nominal rent of £5 a year and lay out the park in a proper manner; and that he should share in the control of the park and have a voice in its regulation. Despite this, in August, the General Purposes Committee recommended that Adderley's offer be declined on the grounds that the terms were not what they had expected. In particular councillors were greatly dissatisfied that Adderley was offering to lease the land and not give it as freehold. Interestingly, Allday was the chairman of the Committee and the Council ratified its decision. Fortunately, Adderley was not to be deterred.

Chapter 2

In the Hands of the People: Adderley Park

Undaunted by the Council's negativity, Adderley responded with a letter to his agent, Mr Couchman, which he asked to be made public in the *'Birmingham Gazette'* on August 27. He made it clear that he had never intimated that he would make a free gift of the ten acres of land for a park to the Council and that his conditions were 'a very reduced rent, a voice in the regulations of the park, and a guarantee of the proper laying out of the ground'.

The rent proposed was at least one-sixth of the real value and was intended more as an acknowledgement than a rent and Adderley maintained that he 'would willingly have reduced it lower still'. As for the stipulation for proper fencing, this 'was not on my own account, but part of a set of park regulations, which they requested me to obtain from Manchester'. Adderley regretted 'that the public should now be deprived of an expected place for recreation, by the offer having failed'.

Accordingly he was resolved to 'myself set apart the same space of ground in the proposed quarter for the public; and as it appears (objections having been made to a fence) that the Committee had no intention of ornamenting the proposed park, such a piece of ground will serve as well all the purposes of a play-ground for all classes of people'. Adderley achieved his aim through an interesting alliance. This included himself, a socially-concerned Tory landowner; skilled working men; and Dawson and others from the Public Recreation Society.

The Society had been formed on December 14, 1855 at a meeting chaired by Mr Brooke Smith. A partner in the manufacturing firm of Martineau and Smith, he had a keen in interest in education for poor children and in the development of freehold land societies. Other speakers included the Reverend J. C. Miller, the rector of St Martin's in the Bull Ring, the parish church of Birmingham. As such he held a leading position, which he enhanced by his involvement in the wider public life. A churchman and Conservative in politics, yet Miller was socially concerned. He was a supporter of education for working-class children and of the Birmingham and Midland Institute, he was also a great friend to local hospitals and had spoken at the meeting about public parks in December 1853.

His brand of paternalistic Toryism was highlighted on that occasion when he had stated that he had lived long enough in Birmingham to know that 'they ought to change their language with regard to the working-classes. They used to consider them as low and grovelling, and to some extent perhaps it was true, but if so it was the fault of the higher classes of society and the ministers of religion'. According to Miller these people should 'have provided better forms of recreation and amusement for the people, and mixed more amongst them' – but he was hopeful that better times were coming.

George Dawson also spoke at this founding meeting of the Public Recreation Society, as did Robert Dale of Carrs Lane Congregational Church. He was another prominent preacher of the Civic Gospel that declared that a great town ought to provide the facilities for the health and welfare of all its citizens, the poor as much as the rich. As such, Dale was also a significant influence upon Joseph Chamberlain and his approach to local government. The final speaker was John Alfred Langford. A writer and journalist later in life, he had benefited from only a few years education before he started working for his father, who was a chair-maker in a small way of business and was one of the many little gaffers in Birmingham.

Langford, however, had a passion for learning and books and as a teenager he had enrolled at the Mechanics' Institute, Birmingham. Although he laboured for fourteen hours each day, he strove to improve his education by learning mathematics, English grammar, Latin, French, and German after work. Following his marriage in 1842, he had lived first in a back house in Bradford Street and then in one in Cheapside, but wherever he lived he maintained his involvement in causes that strove to improve the lives of working-class men and women.

A teetotaller, peace advocate, and a member of a people's library, Langford was keener on social than political agitation. He believed that 'a happy future for man was built on a general, thorough education of the people – the elevation of the masses into men'. The new co-operative movement also attracted him and in 1846 he was appointed honorary secretary of the recently established Birmingham Co-operative Society. The next year he began contributing to *'Howitt's Journal'*, an organ for co-operators.

Then in 1848 Langford began to attend Dawson's Church of the Saviour, continuing to combine his work with his writings and issuing *'Religion, Scepticism and Infidelity in 1850'*. During that winter, he taught evening classes in the schools attached to the Church and gave up chair-making to open a small shop in New Street, selling newspapers and books.

A supporter of radical causes, Langford was a great admirer of Lajos Kossuth, the Hungarian patriot, and in 1851 he became honorary secretary of the Birmingham branch of the 'Friends of Italy', formed to support the Italian patriot Mazzini and his followers. An avid writer of political pamphlets and poetry, Langford was a prime example of a self-taught working man who endeavoured to better himself and his class and his involvement in the Public Recreation Society was just one of his many activities.

After the Society was launched, it soon opened rooms in Great Charles Street. Membership was restricted to those aged eighteen years and above, and the aim was to put on lectures, newspapers, and provide periodicals, vocal and instrumental music, chess, draughts, bagatelle, backgammon, bowls, quoits, skittles, tennis, singlestick, and gymnastics generally. No gambling was allowed; smoking was permitted only in the smoke room; and although refreshments were provided, all intoxicating drinks were excluded. Finally, women were to be admitted to the musical entertainments, lectures, and readings.

Unhappily the Society failed and its rooms were closed late in 1856. However although it was short-lived it was involved in the successful opening of the first public park associated with Birmingham – Adderley Park. In mid-January of that year, Langford and others met Adderley at Saltley to discuss how to progress his offer of gifting ten acres of his land for a public park. It was decided to set up a Working Man's Parks Association, the members of which would elect a committee 'and take the management of the Park into their own hands'.

The Committee was made up of three workmen each from the railway carriage works of Wright's and of Brown and Marshall's in Saltley, and three members of

An illustration of the railway carriage works of Brown and Marshall's in Saltley. Three men from here were on the Working Man's Parks Association that ran Adderley Park in its early years.

the Public Recreation Society – including Langford. Elsewhere in England, public parks were emerging because of the actions either of wealthy men or councils. By contrast, Birmingham was the only place where working-class men were entrusted by a landowner to transform his gift of land into a public park. This was a radical and democratic concept.

Given the longstanding campaign by the working-class for a public park in or near to the town, it was unsurprising that the opening of Adderley Park on Saturday August 30, 1856 was greeted with excitement and joy. By early afternoon of the great day a large crowd had assembled on the east side of the town, ready to walk in procession to Saltley. Their meeting place was around the New Market Hall, erected in 1837 in an area that was rapidly urbanising. Today the site is covered by the dual carriageway of Jennens Row; then it lay in a triangle of land between Prospect Row, AB Row, Cardigan Street, Howe Street and Belmont Row.

Soon after one o'clock, a number of gentlemen arrived. They included the Mayor, Alderman T. R. T. Hodgson, Charles Bowyer Adderley MP himself, and Lord Lyttelton – but by far the greater part of the gathering was working men. The procession set off and was headed by a detachment of the Borough Police. This was followed by the Eighth Troop of the Warwickshire Yeomanry (a forerunner of the Territorial Army) and a band of music attached to Mr Holder of the 'Rodney Inn' of nearby Coleshill Street – a place both of entertainment and drinking and which would be knocked down for the building of the 'Gaiety', Birmingham's first music hall.

Behind Holder's Band came an impressive array of artisans' deputations. They were led by the workers of Saltley, still a largely rural place but one that was set to be transformed into one of the most notable industrial districts in the land famed above all for its railway carriages. And it was the railway carriage workers who were in the forefront of the procession.

First were those of Messrs Brown, Marshall and Co. Originally a stage coach maker, this firm had adapted successfully to the coming of the railways and in 1853 had moved from small premises in New Canal Street to the new and bigger Britannia Works near to Adderley Park. Here the company became celebrated for its luxurious carriages, such as the Peninsular and Oriental Express dining cars completed in 1892 for the line which ran between Calais and Brindisi and which connected the Peninsular and Oriental Steamers. In the twentieth century, the works continued to be well known, but were occupied instead by Morris Commercial.

Next in line were the men of the Saltley Works of Messrs Wright and Company. Joseph Wright was another perceptive stage coach maker who had swiftly recognised the need to move in to making carriages for railways. A Londoner, in 1845 he had relocated his business to six acres just off Saltley Gate as it was close to the two new railway lines entering Birmingham from the east: the Liverpool and Manchester Railway and the Derby Railway, both of which terminated nearby at Curzon Street.

A wonderful floral display at Adderley Park celebrating 100 years of the Council's Parks Department in 1956 – and of course, celebrating 100 years since the Park was opened by the efforts of Charles Bowyer Adderley, later Lord Norton, and local working men.

So rapidly did Wright's concern grow that within two years a further adjoining 50 acres were leased for new industrial development. These Saltley Works soon employed 800 men. They made high-class rolling stock for across the world, carriages that were praised as 'marvels of skilful construction and tasteful decoration'. Wright's later became part of the celebrated Metropolitan Company; whilst from 1853 the Saltley Old Works were let to the London and North Western Railway Company. Their carriage workers were third in line in the procession of artisans' deputations heading for Adderley Park.

Behind them came sword makers from Charles Reeves of Charlotte Street and then, as described in the '*Birmingham Gazette*', 'numerous bodies of the industrious classes in connection with the leading manufactories of the town, with banners, flags, etc'. In their wake came the Provisional Committee for the park, then noblemen and gentlemen, and finally another band. Eye-catching and exuberant, this procession marched brightly and joyously along Ashted Row, down Bloomsbury Street before turning right into Saltley Road so as to cross the River Rea, the canal and railway at Saltley Viaduct.

Thence it was a short distance to the entrance of Adderley Park, where more crowds awaited expectantly. They gave 'a hearty welcome' as the party finally arrived at about 2.00 pm. A salute of guns was fired and then the gates were opened. Within the park there was plenty to do as 'tastefully decorated booths' were set up and games were organised. A tent had also been erected in which 700 guests enjoyed a cold table.

Before they did so, Charles Bowyer Adderley spoke. He paid tribute to Joseph Sturge, who had first proposed that Birmingham should provide pleasure grounds upon the plan adopted in Manchester where the Council had taken the initiative. The idea was that Birmingham should have one great central park as well as a number of pleasure grounds where 'the working men could enjoy themselves after their toil, breathe the fresh air, and have all the benefit which they might otherwise have derived of those smack gardens, of which of late years they had been deprived'.

Adderley believed his gift was more a pleasure ground than a park and he stressed that there were three great fundamental rules upon which its openings was based: 'first that no profit whatever was to be derived from them; secondly, that no money was to be received for admission; and thirdly, that the gates were to be closed at sunset'. The park was not intended for nightly amusement 'but for mid-day recreation and those manly games in which he hoped the people of Birmingham would take pleasure and from which they would derive health and enjoyment'.

Adderley Park was to be managed by a Provisional Committee until a Parks Committee was elected. Indeed Adderley was pleased that the negotiations with the Council had failed because 'it had brought him into a more agreeable relationship with the people'. As a consequence 'the grounds were now entirely in the hands of the people' and Adderley 'looked entirely to the people to keep them in proper order'.

The Parks Committee would endeavour to obtain subscriptions for the efficient maintenance of the Park and they would be in control of the Park's regulations. Adderley hoped that 'the people of Birmingham – men, women and children – might have the full benefit of walking and recreating themselves throughout the grounds on Sunday', but that was a decision for the Committee.

Drawing to the end of his speech, Adderley proposed the health of the Parks Committee and in so doing 'he was proposing the health of the artisans of Birmingham' who were fairly represented by the Committee. From the first its members had met him in a 'high-minded and cordial manner'. They had fully appreciated 'what he had in view, they took it in the right sense, and they evinced the utmost desire to carry out what they saw would be a public benefit'. Importantly it was 'only by co-operation that they could effectually carry out such objects'.

The Committee itself was represented by Henry Priddey, its secretary; Joseph Watson, its treasurer; and Joseph Pinchon, its chairman, who responded to the toast. He explained that 'he and his friends were working men, and it was not immediately their province to make speeches' but he wished to thank the ladies and gentlemen who had responded to the invitation to attend the opening.

Neither the official *'History of the Corporation of Birmingham'* by John Thackray Bunce (volume 2, 1885) nor the important *'Old and New Birmingham'* by Robert K. Dent (1880) mention the working-class campaign for public parks; nor do they refer to the Saltley Park Committee, as it became known. In his *'Modern Birmingham and its Institutions'* (volume 2, 1870) Langford does note the working-men's meeting of June 1853 and the Provisional Committee for managing Adderley Park. Yet like the other two authors he infers that Adderley gave the park to Birmingham in 1856. He did not.

The Saltley Park Committee, as it came to be called, continued to manage affairs for another seven years. However, in late 1862 Adderley decided to lease the ground to the Council for 999 years at a nominal rent of five shillings (25p) a year. His conditions included that it be called Adderley Park; be open to the public all year including Sunday; and be used as a promenade and for cricket, bowls and other athletic sports and not for political meetings or open-air preaching.

The entrance to Adderley Park in 1966; its library was knocked down in the previous year. Lord Norton, the original donor of Adderley Park, continued to support the Park after he handed it to the Council. He added to the equipment and in 1899 gave another acre to the area on the condition that the Council should bear one-third of the expense of making Hams Road on the Park's north-east boundary. This was agreed to.

These stipulations were agreed to by the Council and a vote of thanks was conveyed to Adderley for his 'valuable and philanthropic gesture'. In January 1863 he replied gratefully to the Baths and Parks Committee, but emphasised that he was placing in the hands of the Council a trust 'for the benefit of the public, and the benefit itself is no more than the public ought to have in the neighbourhood of all towns, both for moral and physical welfare'.

It seems that Adderley was motivated by several factors in making his gift. The first was the change in attitude of the Council towards its responsibilities for the citizens of Birmingham. Allday, the chief protagonist of reducing expenditure and minimising local government, had lost his seat on the Council in 1859. Thenceforth the power of the old-style Economists waned. In 1861 their opponents succeeded in pushing for an Improvement Act to sanction borrowing for drainage works; whilst the Council also authorised the opening of two more public baths, the acquisition of land at Witton for the first borough cemetery, and the adoption of a public libraries scheme.

This latter provision was especially important to Adderley as he had also supported the building of a library at the entrance to Adderley Park. It had opened late in 1856 and included a newspaper reading room and a museum. However his gift to Birmingham was also affected by his awareness of the problems faced by the

Children playing in Adderley Park in the 1980s.

Saltley Park Committee, who also managed the library. By the end of March 1863, it owed various tradesmen £270 for expenses incurred in the maintenance of the Park and its Library.

The members were responsible for this debt, which was an unnerving prospect. Skilled workers as they were, yet few would have earned as much as 30 shillings (£1.50) a week. In these circumstances the sum owed was the equivalent of over three years' wages. Fortunately the Council relieved them of their liability, whilst it also took on the two officers in charge of the Park and Library. These were a secretary who was paid £20 year and a park-keeper at 14 shillings (70p) a week. Both had the rent-free accommodation in nearby houses.

On Tuesday January 12, 1864 the *'Birmingham Daily Post'* reported that the previous day, Adderley Park and Free Library had been re-opened to the public 'for the first time since they have been transferred to the guardianship of the Council'. It urged the people of Saltley to make as much use of the facilities as possible as the best method of thanking Adderley for his 'munificent gift'.

Chapter 3

Recreation for the Working Class: Calthorpe Park

Adderley may also have been influenced in gifting Adderley Park to the Council by the success of Calthorpe Park. As early as 1853 Lord Calthorpe, along with Adderley and Sturge, had made a handsome offer for a park. In his case it amounted to 40 acres of 'the most valuable of his land, near the Bristol Road and close up to the town'. The donor, Frederick Gough-Calthorpe, was the fourth Baron Calthorpe and the head of a most fortunate family.

The Goughs were originally from Wolverhampton and had become affluent through that town's important wool trade and later as merchants with the East Indies. They bought the manor of Edgbaston in 1717 and waxed in wealth, all the more so after 1742 when Sir Henry Gough married Barbara Calthorpe – the heiress to wide estates in Norfolk and Hampshire. Their son, Sir Henry Gough-Calthorpe, became the first Baron Calthorpe. Until 1786 he lived in a grand house in Edgbaston surrounded with a park, but then moved to Elvetham Hall in East Anglia. However, Birmingham remained of the utmost importance to family because of the wealth garnered from the Edgbaston Estate.

Soon after the Napoleonic Wars, Sir Henry's third son, George the 3rd Baron Calthorpe, began the development of the area as an exclusive middle-class suburb. This 'Belgravia' of Birmingham, vastly increased his riches and allowed him to benefit from an aristocratic lifestyle; but it also gave him a significant social and political role in Birmingham. It was a role that he took up with vigour.

The third Lord Calthorpe was a keen supporter of the town's petitions to Parliament, at least before the Great Reform Act of 1832 extended the vote to the middle-class; and he was a generous benefactor to many charities and good causes locally. From 1829 he was also a patron and major shareholder of the Birmingham Botanical and Horticultural Society. A year later he went on to lease twelve acres of his land to the society at an advantageous rent. After the Botanical Gardens were opened, it was Lord Calthorpe who complained to the Society in 1838 that its admissions policy was too exclusive and it was he who persuaded it to admit members of the public who were not subscribers on a Monday.

Frederick Gough-Calthorpe succeeded his brother in 1851 as the fourth Lord Calthorpe. Seven years previously he had moved into Perry Hall in Perry Barr, upon his inheritance of the Perry Estate from another branch of the Goughs and lived there until 1862. In the years of his residence he was distinguished by his philanthropy, especially with regard to church building and education. He also renewed the agreement with the Botanical and Horticultural Society and went on to remit its rent of £100 per year; whilst in March 1856 a writer to the *'Birmingham Gazette'* praised his noble example in not building on the last of the guinea gardens in Birmingham. They survive still in Westbourne Road.

Lord Calthorpe's interest in open spaces for the public was made clear by his offer of land for a park in 1853. Yet nothing more was heard of the proposal – although that was unsurprising given the Council's churlish response to Adderley's similarly generous offer two years later. Undaunted Adderley went on to open his pleasure ground, as he called it, and his determination to do so may have spurred on Lord Calthorpe. On April 1, 1856, the General Purposes Committee reported to the Town Council that they had received proposals from him 'for letting to the Corporation, for

A painting by Samuel Lines Senior of the opening of Calthorpe Park. Thanks to Birmingham Museums & Art Gallery.

purposes of public recreation, between twenty and thirty acres of land in the Pershore Road, by way of experiment, for one year, at a rental of £3 per acre'.

Located between the Pershore Road and the River Rea, the land was described in the *'Birmingham Gazette'* as appearing in 'every respect suitable, being in a pleasant and comparatively rural situation, and at the same time contiguous to the centre of the town'. Lord Calthorpe proposed to let it 'for the purpose of recreation for the working-classes, in order to try the effect of it' – but on a number of conditions. Importantly, 'the working-classes shall have free admittance at all hours of the day during the six working days' but the park should be closed on a Sunday.

Moreover 'all gambling, indecent language, and disorderly conduct' were to be strictly prohibited, as were the sale and consumption of 'wine, malt liquor, or spirituous liquors'. There was to be no admittance to horses and carriages, except for chairs on wheels with invalids and children, or to dogs. No games were to be allowed other than cricket, rounders, trap-ball, battledore, quoits, gymnastics, and archery – whilst bathing was explicitly prohibited. Finally a proper number of police officers should be 'in attendance strictly to enforce the above regulations'.

In July 1856 it was reported that the Council, still dominated as it was by the Economists, had replied that it could not legally spend money on the land. In these circumstances the Public Works Committee 'would be happy to receive proposals for the grant of the land in question in perpetuity'. Fortunately Lord Calthorpe did

Crowds around the bandstand in Calthorpe Park in the early 1900s.

Children resting on logs in Calthorpe Park at the turn of the twentieth century. In 1893 access from the Balsall Heath side was improved by the construction of a bridge over the River Rea, and a few years later the park was slightly extended.

not withdraw his offer at what might have been regarded as a disrespectful and arrogant demand. Instead 'he unreservedly gave up the use of the park to them for the use of the inhabitants for twelve months, simply trusting in the Corporation that nothing wrong was done'. The only assurance he sought was that 'the park should be subject to such regulations as were enforced in the parks of other large towns'. In addition Lord Calthorpe explained that he did not mean for the park to be entirely closed on a Sunday, only for games not to be played there on that day.

As for the Council, it agreed to provide police for the park and to lay it out. By the late spring of 1857 it had been made ready. Consisting of five meadows made into one, the park was intersected by gravel paths and planted with a variety of bushes. On May 29, 1857 the *'Morning Chronicle'* in London reported that 'great preparations were in progress' for a general holiday on the opening of Calthorpe Park the following Monday by Prince George, the Duke of Cambridge. A cousin of Queen Victoria, he was the commander in chief of the British army and had served a few years previously in the Crimean War. According to the *'Worcester Journal'* because of his presence the opening was to be 'celebrated in festival fashion. Most house-holders on the line of procession have intimated their intention of decorating their premises; and others will erect triumphal arches'.

As it was, the event gained notice in newspapers across the country. After arriving by train at Snow Hill Station, the Duke was received by the Mayor, John Ratcliff, and some councillors. Thence he was taken to the Town Hall for a private luncheon, after which he entered the main part of the building where there was a large assembly of the local middle-class. After several speeches, the official party left for Calthorpe Park. Amongst others, the *'Wells Journal'*, reported that to describe the rout 'would be but to picture a continued scene of ovation. From every window and every parapet streamed forth the gayest banners'.

At intervals the Duke passed under handsomely decorated triumphal arches. All the way he was cheered by countless thousands who lined the streets, whilst eager sightseers filled every available inch of standing room in houses and buildings that he passed. From New Street the procession went through the Bull Ring and Digbeth,

Park keepers at the entrance to Calthorpe Park on the corner of the Pershore Road and Speedwell Road in about 1900. By the mid-1880s, Birmingham's Parks and Gardens were looked after by a staff of one superintendent at a salary of £250 a year; and 45 park keepers and gardeners, paid a total of £2,452. The first superintendent was Alfred Rodway, who held the post for many years.

Police officers at Calthorpe Park in the Edwardian period.

along Bromsgrove Street and Bristol Street to Speedwell Road and the park, where cannon were fired in the Duke's honour. People 'covered every plot of land as far as the eye could reach', apart from where the official group was gathered. Here three cedars trees were planted: one each by the Duke, Lord Calthorpe, and the Mayor.

After announcing that formal possession of the park had been taken, the Duke was taken two miles, through more cheering crowds, to the Mayor's house. That evening he was entertained at a magnificent banquet at Dee's Hotel, attended by 250 members of the aristocracy, gentry and upper middle-classes. At the same time a free concert was put on at the Town Hall for artisans, their wives and families; a free ball was held at the Music Hall in Coleshill Street; and a free meal was given to 700 soldiers and pensioners at Bingley Hall.

All of the considerable expenses of the day were paid for by the Mayor, John Ratcliff. He was a partner with his brother, Charles, in a highly successful factory that

Children playing on make-shift swings with tyres on the Edward Road side of Calthorpe Park in the late 1970s. From its beginnings, the greater part of the Calthorpe Park was open. This made it popular with children and also a favourite place of resort for cricket and football clubs.

made lamps, chandeliers, candelabras, bronzes, inkstands, vases, and gas fittings. Having made his fortune by his middle age, Ratcliff entered public life fully. It was well that he was wealthy for as the *'Wells Journal'* noted wryly, his liberality arose from 'fearing probably the tightness of the municipal purse strings'. Apparently, the miserliness of Birmingham's Economist councillors was widely known.

Calthorpe Park was recognised as the second park for the people of Birmingham. For several years it was mostly maintained as an open field, after which a new lodge, entrance gates and refreshment room were provided whilst ornamental iron palisading was put up along the Pershore Road frontage. Proper walks and shrubberies were also formed, but according to John Thackray Bunce in the *'History of the Corporation of Birmingham'*, the greater part of the ground was kept open, and it became 'a favourite place of resort for cricket and football clubs. It also serves as an exercising ground for the Rifle Volunteers; being perfectly level, it is admirably suited for these purposes'.

As for the tenure of Calthorpe Park, this was unsettled for many years. Although the Town Council became its occupiers in 1857 this was only by permission of Lord Calthorpe and not by any legal document. Bunce emphasised that the Council 'were occupiers on sufferance, paying a nominal rent of £5'. In 1870, the fifth Lord Calthorpe offered to grant a lease of the land for 21 years – this being the longest term that he had the power to give as a life-holder of the Edgbaston Estate. As such he also had to charge a fair annual value of £300, but this would be with an honourable understanding on his part that £295 should be returned to the Council.

This offer was declined as it would not allow the Council to spend money on the park. Consequently the Baths and Parks Committee sought an interview with Lord Calthorpe. On August 22, 1871, it reported that Lord Calthorpe and his two brothers had generously agreed to a deed of renunciation which 'enabled his lordship to make a grant of the land to the Corporation for the purpose to which it had been dedicated'. By this date the Council was in full possession of its third public park – Aston Park. Its acquisition was long-drawn out but owed much to the resolve of the working-class and their supporters.

Chapter 4

Free to All: Aston Park

'Fête Champêtre at Aston Hall' – it was a fancy name for a grand event in a splendid setting that was held on Monday, July 27, 1856. More prosaically it was a huge garden party to raise funds for the Queen's Hospital in Bath Row. Queen Victoria herself and her husband, Prince Albert were amongst the long list of royal and aristocratic patrons – although they did not attend. Advertisements for the fête declared that it would be held in the 'beautiful park and grounds of the ancient baronial mansion', and the *'Worcester Chronicle'* proclaimed it as 'a wondrous success'. So it was. Nearly 50,000 people paid one shilling (5p) to attend and after paying out entertainment expenses, the Committee was able to pass over the sizeable sum of £2,329.

In his fascinating account of *'Personal Recollections of Birmingham and Birmingham Men'* (1877), Eliezer Edwards recounted how the memorable event had come about. The 'Woodman' in Easy Row was an inn popular with councillors, aldermen, manufacturers and more prosperous shopkeepers. Amongst the regulars was the glass manufacturer and soda water producer, John Walsh Walsh. He was also a councillor and compared with many others 'much might be said of the energetic manner in which he opposed all weakness in action, and of the manly vigour of his advocacy of all schemes for the benefit of the town'.

In particular, he had worked hard 'to induce the Council to buy Aston Park for the town, when its price was low'; and in later years, he would 'chafe at the thought that double the present area of the park might have been purchased, for less money than was ultimately paid for the portion now held'. One spring evening in 1856, he was in the 'Woodman' and led a discussion on the Council's folly 'in refusing to buy a portion of Aston Park, including the Hall, which had been offered to them, as he said, "dirt cheap"'.

Another member of the group mentioned that the financial affairs of the Queen's Hospital 'were in a lamentable state of collapse'. Hearing this Walsh announced 'why not borrow the park and give a picnic for the hospital?' A decisive man, 'with him, to conceive was to act'. Within days, a provisional committee with Walsh as chairman was appointed and a deputation was sent to the proprietors of the park. They granted permission to hold a fête.

Walsh energetically took up the matter and resolved it would be no mere picnic but 'such a fête as Birmingham had never witnessed, and would not readily forget'; nor did it. Huge numbers of tickets were sold and as the day approached:

The refreshment contractors were advised of the vastly increased number of hungry customers they might expect. Bakers were set to work to provide hundreds of additional loaves. Orders were given for an extra ton or two of sandwiches. Scores more barrels of ale and porter came slowly into the park, where, within fenced enclosures, they were piled, two or three high, in double lines. Crates upon crates of tumblers, earthenware mugs, and plates arrived. Soda water, lemonade, and ginger beer were provided in countless grosses, and in fact everything for the comfort and convenience of visitors that the most careful forethought could suggest, was provided in the most lavish profusion.

Monday July 28 was 'delightfully fine' and was taken as a general holiday locally. Aston Village was gaily decorated, the Royal Standard floated from its parish church – whilst its bells 'chimed out in joyous melody'. The Elizabethan gateway to the park was hung with bunting and 'the sober old Hall had a sudden eruption of colour, such as it had probably never known before'. Flags of all colours were everywhere and as noon approached, train after train 'deposited at the Aston station hundreds and thousands of gaily-attired Black Country people'. To their number were added the hosts that came from Birmingham on special trains or who were crammed into 'omnibuses, waggons, cabs, carts, and every other imaginable vehicle; whilst thousands upon thousands of dusty pedestrians jostled each other in the crowded roads'.

Aston Hall was thrown open, and outside there were platforms for dancing, pavilions for musicians, swings, merry-go-rounds, Punch and Judy shows, games and other amusements. Importantly:

> All classes were represented at the fête. Here you might see a group of well-dressed folks from Edgbaston, next some pale-faced miners from the Black Country, and then the nut-brown faces of some agricultural people. All seemed intent upon fun and pleasure, and so, throughout that long summer day, the crowd increased, and everyone seemed to be in a state of absolute enjoyment.

In the evening the Sycamore Avenue was lighted up by innumerable coloured lamps to conjure a fairylike scene and 'then came the fireworks! No such display had ever before been seen in the Midland Counties. The nights of rockets, the marvellously-ingenious set pieces, and the wonderful blue lights, gave intense delight'. The finale was as spectacular; the words 'SAVE ASTON HALL' came out in glowing fire to the acclaim of the vast crowd.

The remarkable achievement of the first Aston Fête encouraged Walsh and his committee to organise another 'Grand Fête Champêtre' for the General Hospital in Summer Lane, which they boasted would surpass the Queen's Hospital event.

Boys on what looks like a type of climbing frame in the early 1900s. This and another set of 'gymnastic apparatus', as they were called, were donated in 1900 by Edward Ansell, of the family of Aston brewers. The previous year, Frederick Smith, a member of another firm of Aston brewers, had gifted the park with a band-stand. Following Ansell's example, the Council constructed a similar open-air gymnasium in Calthorpe Park.

Amongst the entertainers would be 'the orchestral union band of thirty of the most eminent instrumentalists of the day'; the far-famed and superb band of the Royal Artillery Corps; 200 of the Birmingham Orchestral Society; 'the splendid band' of the 10th Hussars; 'the justly celebrated band' of Chance's Brothers in Smethwick; the Worcestershire Band; Harvey and Synyer's 'celebrated six-horn band'; and five quadrille bands.

There was also 'a grand archery meeting'; illuminations in the Sycamore Avenue consisting of 30,000 'variegated lamps'; and 'a magnificent display of fireworks on a scale of grandeur unsurpassed by any previous exhibition in the kingdom' supplied by the Royal Arsenal in Woolwich. Tents for wines, spirits and refreshments were put up that were capable of holding 40,000 people.

Fortunately that Monday September 15, the weather was fine and it was reported that double that figure attended. So excited was Birmingham and the district at this second fête and so good was the charitable cause that employers happily closed large factories and works. The *'Birmingham Gazette'* reported that 'the demand for every description of vehicular accommodation was something extraordinary to witness'; whilst the special trains laid on from the mining districts 'were literally packed with eager pleasure seekers'.

Within Birmingham, it was as if 'the whole population seemed on the move'. There was an unbroken procession from Dale End along all the roads that led to Aston and soon 'the town began to wear a deserted appearance, showing unmistakably that Birmingham had made up its mind for once to indulge in a holiday'. According to the *'Morning Chronicle'* the neighbourhood of Birmingham was 'the scene of great gaiety and high festivity'. The London-based newspaper went on to stress that two miles from the town centre, Aston Hall was surrounded by a well-wooded park, interspersed with stately avenues and was an admirable place for a fête champêtre. So it was but that wonderful setting was under threat.

Aston Hall had been built for Sir Thomas Holte between 1618 and 1635. A magnificent Jacobean mansion with wide lands, it was inherited by the last of his name, Mary Holte. She was married to Abraham Bracebridge of Atherstone, but unhappily he was spectacularly irresponsible and a failure in his business affairs. In anticipation of his wife inheriting the Holte property, Abraham Bracebridge used them to raise mortgages. By 1798, he owed the massive sum of £55,000 and oblivious to his shortcomings he continued to make disastrous financial decisions.

Unable to discharge his loans, in 1818 he obtained an Act of Parliament allowing the partition and sale of the Holte lands to raise funds to pay his creditors. Aston Hall and about 327 acres of parkland were bought by a firm of Warwick bankers. They leased it to James Watt the younger, the son of the celebrated engineer, who lived there until 1848. His departure signalled the development of much of the parkland. Building plots were sold and new roads were quickly cut.

The imminent disappearance of the last of the park seems to have energised some of Birmingham's councillors who were more committed to providing facilities for the people they represented than were the Economists. Alderman J. H. Cutler was chief amongst them. Still battling away against the prevailing misers, in August 1856 he moved in the Town Council that the General Purposes Committee be authorised to communicate with the proprietors of the Aston Park Estate to ascertain upon what terms it might be 'acquired as a public park and place of recreation for the inhabitants of the town'.

Cutler explained that he had been approached by one of the proprietors who had 'expressed an anxiety that the park should be possessed by the Council, as this was the only means by which it could be maintained in its present state of entirety'. Alderman Cutler pointed out that six years before the Council had made inquiries about the park but it had not been able to proceed because of the cost and the Council then had no power to borrow money for such a purpose. Now it did thanks to the Birmingham Parks Act of 1854. This authorised borrowing up to £30,000, a sum that could be supplemented by a rate of one penny per property per year so as to purchase a park.

Alderman Cutler did not believe that the proprietors would ask an exorbitant amount for Aston Hall and a certain amount of the park. He emphasised that the people of Birmingham felt 'a deep interest in the preservation of the building, and he would go still further and say a deep interest in becoming possessed of it for the benefit of the inhabitants generally'. Much had spoken about gin palaces and their demoralising effects and in his opinion 'if they wished effectually to remove these evils and empty them of their visitors they must provide the people with other and more rational pursuits. Give them a museum and a good Park and he felt confident these advantages would do much towards weaning them from grosser amusements'.

Moreover, Cutler was certain that Aston Park would 'afford the opportunity for carrying out projects in aid of their charitable institutions, most of which were in a state of poverty'. This had been made clear by the recent fête for the Queen's Hospital, an event that had also shown that 'immense assemblages could meet without drunkenness or damage to property being the result'.

Interestingly Alderman Allday, the high priest of Council frugality supported the motion. It was likely that this was because he and his supporters had been denigrated for their lack of activity in providing parks – and, of course, Adderley Park was due to be opened soon, on August 30 thanks to the benevolence of Charles Bowyer Adderley. Allday's statement suggested self-interest, for 'he hoped the resolution would be carried unanimously, so that the noblemen and gentlemen connected with the town would see that the Council desired to co-operate with them in providing places of recreation for the people'.

In December the General Purposes Committee reported that the proprietors wanted £24,500 for Aston Hall and 30 acres of parkland; and £36,400 for an additional 52 acres selected by the Committee as the most eligible. Unfortunately a surveyor engaged by the Council valued the 82 acres at only £23,000 and the 172 acres that were left of the original Park at £50,000. Toing and froing between the council and the proprietors continued but matters were soon to be taken out of the hands of the local authority by the people.

The day after the first 'Fête Champêtre' for the Queen's Hospital, the redoubtable and visionary preacher George Dawson had launched a 'Save Aston Hall' campaign in the *'Daily Press'*. Started only the year before, this was the first daily newspaper in the town. Dawson was a chief shareholder whilst John Henry Langford was a sub-editor. In his article, Dawson urged the public to raise the money to purchase Aston Hall and Park, and in the subsequent months his appeal was printed as a handbill and posted on all the blank walls in and around the town.

The appeal roused a group of 'gentlemen' to action. On May 20, 1857, they held a private meeting at which they suggested the formation of a company, which would raise the necessary capital to buy Aston Hall and part of the park through the purchase of shares that would cost a small amount each. A subsequent meeting was held on June 30. It was chaired by Charles Holte Bracebridge, the son of Mary Holte and Abraham Bracebridge. He was the antithesis of his father. A clever and caring man, he was involved in prison reform and he and his wife played a vital role in helping Florence Nightingale in the Crimean War. Bracebridge was a crucial figure in saving the home of his ancestors and in providing part of its grounds as a park for the people.

At this meeting it was resolved that it was 'desirable to purchase 43 acres of land in Aston Park, including timber and the Hall, for the sum of £35,000'. To these ends a company should be formed. A prospectus followed quickly. It proposed to raise £42,000 by the sale of 40,000 shares at £1 1s each (£1.05). The aim was 'that Aston Hall may ultimately become free to all'. Crucially, the promoters of the company proclaimed that they were 'actuated by a desire to preserve from destruction the venerable edifice of Aston Hall, with its historic associations, and at the same time to afford to the town the advantages of a park and place of recreation and amusement'.

Unhappily, as Langford described, 'somehow the thing was not enthusiastically taken up. One promoter after another resigned. The machine did not run well'. Then someone was inspired to make an appeal to the working-class. Workers at the

Another smashing photo, this time of girls at what seems to be a maypole in the early 1900s.

leading manufactories were invited to send delegates to a meeting on June 26, 1857 in the committee room of the Town Hall. George Dawson was called to the chair and Langford reported proudly that 'the meeting was unanimous and enthusiastic; the object was approved'. A committee was appointed with Dawson as chairman, Langford as vice-chairman, and Daniel J. O'Neill as honorary secretary.

A Dubliner who had settled in Birmingham, O'Neill was hailed in his obituary in the *'Birmingham Gazette'* on July 21, 1914 as 'The Friend of the Poor' and 'as one of the most interesting personalities in the public and social life of Birmingham for upwards of half a century'. From when he first entered public life there were few movements with which 'he was not connected in some way, or other. He was a friend to all, especially the "little prisoners in the slums" and was respected by all classes of the community'.

O'Neill had come to Birmingham from Ireland in 1852 as a young man of twenty. A silver smith and art metal worker, he had gained an important clerical position at R. W. Winfield's in Cambridge Street – now the site of the Library of Birmingham. Winfield's was one of the most important firms in the city and its workers had sent representatives to the first meeting called by workers to campaign for public parks in 1853.

In his publication, *'How Aston Hall and Park Were Saved'* (1910) O'Neill stated that he became involved in the campaign 'to endeavour to get Birmingham a Park worthy of the name; to save a grand historic building from being carted away, as so many thousands of old bricks; and to prevent the magnificent trees being felled for jerry-building and road. The grand building was Aston Hall'.

Langford stressed that from the first working-men's meeting the work of saving Aston Hall and Park 'may be said to have begun in earnest'. Their committee members quickly found that 'there was no active organisation, and that there was no money for carrying out the preliminary business of starting and enrolling a company'. Consequently they called a public meeting, employed canvassers, gave talks, and arranged for a fête to be held at the Park to raise the funds for the purchase.

This was held on August 17, 1857. Unhappily the attendance was disappointingly low and it produced a profit of £569 11s. ld, which was considerably lower than the sums raised for the local hospitals at their fêtes. Langford regretted that the working-class, 'for whose especial benefit the project of purchasing was devised', had not given 'a very encouraging amount of support, or displayed an inordinate amount of enthusiasm on the occasion'. Still the sum was a large one 'and the working men deserved the warm congratulations of all for the tact and energy with which they began their labours'.

Yet it seemed that the plan to save Aston Hall and Park once again was 'in deadly peril'. Immediately after the fête the proprietors ended negotiations, stating that the time that they had allowed the original promoters of the company to reach an agreement to purchase had now elapsed. The working men were undaunted and took 'prompt and decisive action'. In September they sent a deputation to speak with the owners, who agreed that negotiations could be renewed. There was one important proviso, though: the terms were to be the same as before.

This meant a price of £35,000 for the hall and 43 acres of park, although the proprietors agreed to take £4,200 worth of shares instead of money upon the completion of the contract. By the end of 1857, a deposit of £3,500 had to be paid over and the company had to take possession. Two years were then allowed for completing the purchase, with the money owed to be paid in quarterly instalments of £4,000.

The Working-Men's Committee agreed and suggested their body should amalgamate with the original promoters of the company. Langford was appointed secretary of the new committee which included Dawson, Bracebridge and fourteen other 'gentlemen'. Their number was matched by working men and this committee became the interim managers. The company was registered with the simple object of purchasing Aston Hall and Park as a place of recreation and amusement. The contract was then signed with the proprietors and a deposit of £3,500 paid on February 12, 1858. Four days later the Aston Hall and Park Company Limited took possession of the property.

It was aimed to raise £42,000 through the sale of 40,000 guinea (£1.05p) shares payable by half-crown instalments. 'A' shareholders would be admitted to the Park and Hall on all ordinary occasions, including Sundays, Good Fridays, Christmas Days, and legally appointed holidays, but they would not be entitled to dividends or admission either to extraordinary fêtes or charitable or public events.

'B' shares were donations and not to entitle the donors to privileges or profits. Instead the money was to be vested in trustees for the purpose of eventually making the Park free. Finally, 'C' shareholders were entitled to dividends, but not to privileges. Salaried officers were to be elected annually. They would include a manager who 'would provide museums, exhibitions, concerts, lectures, fêtes, and to do all things that may forward the objects of the company'.

It was expected that the shares would be redeemed out of the profits of refreshments and entertainments, and that this would then allow the transfer of Aston Hall and Park to the Corporation. With this in mind, on March 9, Langford applied to the Council for the appointment of four councillors as Borough Trustees. It was referred to the General Purposes Committee, who in turn appointed a sub-committee to investigate the issue. The result was a lengthy document which recommended that the application be refused.

Before the Council could do so formally, the Company withdrew its offer in mid-April 1858. The Council was still dominated by those motivated only by lowering costs and by enforcing a policy of economy through efficiency. This meant

An inspection of Aston Park by the Parks Committee in 1926. Until 1911, the administration of Birmingham's parks came under the Baths and Parks Committee; in that year, however, the two elements were separated. Thenceforth the Parks Committee held annual inspections of each park.

Two years before this photo was taken the Birmingham Civic Society had re-planned a large area of the park. It also carried out the work with the Parks Department, ensuring that the gardens would reflect the style that may have been contemporary to the Hall. This approach ensured that the gardens had views to the east and west fronts.

that councillors would not take on a project that may have cost money even if it were for the well-being of its citizens.

By now Langford was share and donation manager. He was replaced as secretary by O'Neill, who had resigned his position at Winfield's. O'Neill reported on behalf of the Interim Managers at the first shareholders' meeting at the Town Hall on March 30. It was well attended with between 400-500 people present, most of whom were working men, and several speakers announced to cheers that Aston Park was to become a Free Park, a People's Park.

O'Neill indicated that from the first the Working Men's Committee had 'a strong feeling upon the necessity of making an extraordinary display at the opening of the Park'. As soon as 'the success of the movement was placed beyond a doubt, the working men thought if a proper representation was made to her Most Gracious Majesty of the purposes for which the park and hall were adapted, and the means by which they were obtained, her Majesty might be pleased to accept an invitation to inaugurate the People's Park'. O'Neill was certain that this honour was 'the crowning success of their undertaking'.

The Mayor, John Ratcliff, had undertaken the initial steps and to the surprise of many, Queen Victoria had accepted the invitation. Robert K. Dent believed that she did so because she was persuaded that the company was in effect 'an association originated by the working-classes for the purpose of acquiring a Park, the ultimate destination of which is, that it shall be free for the inhabitants of the Borough'.

Langford and others on the committee were keen that Aston Hall itself should become 'the great pattern card of all our artistic and manufacturing skill, a perpetual exhibition of the works of our manufacturers and artists'. To that end, for the Queen's visit, there was to be an exhibition of fine arts in the building itself. Sir Francis Scott of Great Barr Hall made an appeal on their behalf.

Published in the *'Birmingham Gazette'* on April 19, it praised the working men of Birmingham for their united action and 'energetic canvassing and unsparing sacrifice of time and exertion of many men of influence among their body'. Aided by the contributions of local gentlemen they had purchased Aston Hall, and 'thereby rescued from destruction one of the most picturesque and unaltered of our Jacobean buildings; and with it secured the possession of the terrace, gardens, and about forty acres of the beautifully situated and well-timbered Park'.

Scott also urged not only the loan of artefacts and paintings but also financial contributions to the company 'as not being entered into with a view to the profit of a few, but for the permanent benefit of the entire Working Class of Birmingham'. It was intended to form a comprehensive Museum of Fine Arts and Manufactures in Aston Hall, and a glass building attached to it, which was to be built, 'so that while the beautiful grounds will afford a place of innocent bodily recreation to the artisan and his family, his mind may, at the same time, gather materials from the observation of nature, and the study of works of art, wherewith to improve his taste, correct his design, and render him (as all experience justifies me in asserting) both a better man and a better workman'.

The great day itself was Tuesday June 15 1858. It was the first time a reigning monarch had visited Birmingham officially. Given the egalitarian nature of the town's citizens and their longstanding and steadfast support for democratic campaigns, some of the upper-class locally and nationally were worried at the reception that the Queen and Prince Albert would receive. But even 'The Times' had to concede that 'dark insinuations of danger' were an atrocious libel on the people of Birmingham. They acclaimed the Queen enthusiastically, a theme picked up by the *'Morning Post'*.

Its correspondent affirmed that 'Manchester, Liverpool and Edinburgh have boasted the loyal expenditure in welcoming the sovereign's occasional visits, but it has been reserved for the "Queen of the Midland Counties" to show what could be accomplished when good taste and unsparing zeal combined to offer a loyal reception to Her Majesty, upon the occasion of her first visit to the neighbourhood'. Indeed there may have been as equally gratifying displays of loyal affection elsewhere 'but assuredly none ever worked harder or more effectively than the loyal inhabitants of Birmingham, which for once put on holiday attire, and lost for a period its reputed work day and sombre character'.

A reporter for the 'Globe' was as fulsome in his praise for the Queen's welcome by half a million people 'gathered from the great city and the adjacent districts'. The last time a sovereign had come close to Birmingham was in the English Civil War, when Charles I had stayed at Aston Hall. He left to fight the Battle of Edgehill and 'Birmingham sallied forth and laid siege to the royalist stronghold'. By contrast, multitudes now lined the streets whilst 'the house-fronts and house-tops were alive with warm-hearty subjects'.

As the *'Manchester Examiner'* revealed, large sums of money were spent by the principal tradesmen and residents in dressing up the fronts of their premises. Even in the back streets, every shop and dwelling had at least a flagpole or a bit of bunting. Everywhere was a cacophony of joyful noise, the lusty cheers of the onlookers vying for supremacy with 'the musical clangour from many a steeple and tower' and with the strains of military and other bands.

A gardener at work on the flower beds in front of Aston Hall in the 1950s.

Queen Victoria arrived by rail just after 12 noon, and was escorted to a reception at the Town Hall, where the Mayor presented a loyal address to her. The Queen replied that:

> It is most gratifying to me to have the opportunity of visiting this ancient and enterprising town, the centre of so much of our manufacturing industry; and I trust you may long remain in the full enjoyment of that liberty and security without which even industry itself must fail to reap its appropriate reward.
>
> I desire you will convey to the vast community which you represent, my sincere thanks for their cordial welcome, assuring them at the same time of the pleasure I have derived from witnessing the great and increasing prosperity of Birmingham and its neighbourhood.

After a second address to Prince Albert and his response, the Queen knighted the Mayor. Sir John Ratcliff then escorted her to Aston Hall. The *'Morning Herald'* was thrilled that over the two-mile journey 'the streets presented the appearance of a grand floral arcade – every house had its flags and ensigns, and at intervals the scene was rendered the more imposing by the erection of grand triumphal arches, upon the decorations of which neither time nor expense had been spared'. Many newspapers commentated particularly upon the gunmakers' arch.

For the *'Liverpool Daily Post'* the most important feature was the preservation of Aston Hall and its noble grounds as 'a public park and museum for the people'. If Liverpool could proudly boast of a great public benefactor in William Brown, then Birmingham, too, 'can turn with pride to the munificence of a private individual, whose chief characteristic is to be the fit representative of a numerous class – a working man grown rich by industry'.

This theme was brought to the fore at Aston Hall in the address to the Queen by Sir Francis Scott. He stressed that:

> in some towns in your Majesty's dominions public parks have wisely been provided by wealthy Corporations; in others by the munificence of philanthropic citizens; here, also, we are indebted to private liberality for two places of recreation for the people but to Birmingham alone has it been given to secure by her own exertions an ancient Park for the physical relaxation – an ancient Hall for the mental cultivation – of her variously employed and laborious population.
>
> Your Majesty will, we believe, be gratified to learn that Aston Hall and Park have been acquired for the most part by the industry and economy of the people themselves. Of the money required for this purpose a very large proportion has been subscribed by the working-classes, a circumstance which we venture to hope will not be without interest and satisfaction to your Majesty.

Four of the interim managers were presented to the Queen. They were W. Lucy, T. Lloyd, J. P. Turner, and J. A. Langford. Her Majesty also 'showed her appreciation of the part which the working men had taken in this work by having Messrs T. Twiss, G. Tarplee, C. Hawkesford, H. G. Quilter, H. Bourne, M. Lees, D. J. O'Neill, and S. Partridge, all members of the committee, called before her'. She recognised 'with pleasure the labour you have undertaken in providing thus worthily for the physical and intellectual improvement of the working-classes, and I sincerely hope that this Hall and Park will prove a boon and a comfort to the people of Birmingham'. After more presentations, Queen Victoria passed from the grand gallery to the balcony. She was received with the most deafening of cheers by the assembled thousands and then pronounced the park open.

Regrettably, following the royal visit both the public take-up of shares and donations dropped off, whilst some existing shareholders failed to keep up their payments. The managers of Aston Hall and Park realised that a large amount of money was needed soon to keep up the disbursements to the vendors. Thomas Lloyd, a banker from the wealthy family that founded Lloyd's Bank and a keen Liberal, was treasurer of the Company. In December 1858, he approached the Mayor, Sir John Ratcliff, to lead a campaign to raise £10,000 and to make a significant contribution himself.

As for Lloyd he would gift £1,000. He felt that none could refuse such an appeal for 'with a little self-sacrifice we shall perform our promise to the Queen; for everyone who took part in the reception of the Queen did promise to make Aston Park a Free Park'. Lloyd had one condition. The whole venture had been 'a workman's affair, and the workmen have done well; but I would make the payment of the subscriptions depend upon the co-operation of the employed, and their subscribing half the amount required'.

Despite the fact that he had been knighted because of the Queen's visit to Aston Hall and Park, Sir John Ratcliff failed to take up the challenge. The response was as muted from the general public. A canvassing committee was then appointed which organised a highly successful fête in July 1859. It raised almost £2,000 but problems continued. Too few people bought shares, or could afford to do so; mismanagement led to lower profits from big events; several thousand pounds had been spent on repairs and decorations to Aston Hall; and as Langford, stressed 'with a few honourable exceptions, wealthy citizens were conspicuously absent in their support'.

By early 1861, the new Council for Aston Hall and Park had the difficult task of renegotiating terms with the vendors as it was impossible for them to make the required payments. In an effort to make money quickly, the famed tightrope artiste Blondin was engaged to make his first appearance in Birmingham at a two-day fête on June 8 and 9, 1861. Nearly £2,000 profit was made, but this only allowed a payment of £1,080 interest to the proprietors and £920 on account of the purchase.

A similar fête was held the next year, but Langford recorded gloomily that 'the attractions of Blondin were no more what they had been. The first keen edge of excitement was gone, and the fête was a comparative failure'. It raised only £200. The general working of the Company was good, but the amount owing was too great to make a dent in the amount owed. Then in 1863 there came a crisis. The Forester's Fête on July 20 featured 'the Female Blondin (Mrs Powell)'. Tragically, as she was performing on the high rope it broke 'and the poor woman was killed on the spot'.

This terrible accident prompted the Queen to have a letter written on July 25 to the Mayor, Charles Sturge, the brother of Joseph, the campaigner for peace and working-class rights. She wanted to make known 'her personal feelings of horror that one of her subjects, a female, should have been sacrificed to the gratification of the demoralising taste unfortunately prevalent for exhibitions attended with the greatest danger to the performers'.

A superb view of industrial east Birmingham from the vantage point of Aston Hall. In the foreground a gardener works on the flower beds; on the left is Aston Parish Church; and on the right are the gas works in Nechells Place.

Such exhibitions were deemed demoralising, and the Queen trusted that the Mayor, 'in common with the rest of the townspeople of Birmingham, will use your influence to prevent in future the degradation to such exhibitions of the Park which was gladly opened by her Majesty and the beloved Prince Consort, in the hope that it would be made serviceable for the healthy exercise and rational recreation of the people'.

Chastened, the Mayor hastened to give the Queen 'my humble assurance that there is not in the kingdom an individual who laments more sincerely than myself, not only the melancholy accident to which you refer, but the depraved taste for a barbarous species of amusement which unhappily has become popular, not only in the Metropolis, but in all parts of her Majesty's home dominions'.

As for the future, although Aston Park was beyond Birmingham's jurisdiction, he hoped that 'their influence and that of their fellow townsmen, will henceforth limit its use exclusively to the healthy exercise and rational recreation of the people, so that the gracious intentions of her Majesty and her revered Consort may not be frustrated but realised'.

The Secretary of State, Sir George Grey, also addressed a letter to the Managers of the Company expressing his 'hope that after this melancholy occurrence you will not allow a repetition of such dangerous performances in the Park'. The managers concurred with these sentiments and stated they had 'endeavoured, as far as possible, to provide healthful recreation and instruction for the people'. On this particular occasion the Park had been let for a charitable purpose and the managers had not reserved any right to control the performances.

It was now obvious that Aston Hall and Park could not be bought by the Company – in spite of the best efforts of all concerned. Only £9,000 of the purchase money of £35,000 had been paid; and it was feared that if the company collapsed, as was a possibility, that Aston Hall and Park would be lost to the people forever. The Managers realised this and on August 4 sent a resolution to the same Council meeting at which the Queen's letter was read out. It stated that they were 'desirous that steps should be taken to arrange with the Corporation for the completion of the purchase'.

Allday, the chief protagonist of the economists, had lost his position on the Council four years before, in 1859, yet still the Council was characterised by lethargy. It dithered and prevaricated; worse than that, according to the *'Birmingham Daily Post'*, the application from the Managers 'was received coldly'. It was referred to the Baths and Parks Committee – a grand title for a body that oversaw only two parks, both of which had been donated to the town by benefactors. Moreover the motion in favour of acceding to the proposal was rejected by 40 votes to 11.

On October 8, the Mayor then wrote to Lord Leigh in the latter's capacity as Lord Lieutenant of Warwickshire – given that Aston was not then part of

Birmingham and was a parish in that county. The Mayor stressed that 'unless means are used, without delay, to secure the property in perpetuity for the rational recreation of the people, possession will be resumed by its former owners'. This would be a catastrophe and could only be averted if Aston Hall and Park were vested in a responsible public body, in particular the Corporation of Birmingham. It would cost £28,000 'to effect this desirable object', on top of which 'a considerable additional outlay must be incurred in fencing, restoration, and otherwise, to render the Hall and Park suitable for the contemplated purpose'.

Ironically given the Council's longstanding antipathy to providing municipal public parks and its ill-favoured reputation for procrastination, the Mayor declared that 'redemption is even now not impossible, if prompt and energetic measures be adopted'. He believed that the money could be raised by the combined efforts of the Corporation, Lord Leigh and the justices and gentlemen of Warwickshire; 'in short, if the County will move in the matter promptly and energetically, as they will I am sure on your Lordship's call, I will move the Council for a vote of £20,000, and I am satisfied I shall not move in vain'.

Lord Leigh did indeed approach the magistracy of Warwickshire to call a meeting to raise the £8,000 sought by the Mayor. They deemed it inadvisable to do so. The Mayor had their decision conveyed to the Queen. Now alerted to the ominous situation of the Park she had opened, in early November 1864 she instructed another letter to be sent to the Mayor. It was strongly worded and in effect chastised the Council for its lack of action. The Queen regretted:

> very much to hear that there exists a possibility of the people of Birmingham losing the enjoyment of Aston Park as a place of healthy exercise and recreation. In such a hive of industry, an open area for relaxation and amusement after toil must be most valuable.
>
> Her Majesty had hoped that this requirement had been permanently provided for; and Her Majesty is still unwilling to believe that, in a locality in which so much wealth is found in proximity to the hard labour by which it is produced, funds can be wanting to secure to the population an enjoyment to value.

The intervention of the Queen and the bad publicity that it engendered for Birmingham stirred a group of philanthropic men to do something. They included longstanding supporters of public parks such as Thomas Lloyd and the Reverend Dr Miller of St Martin's. Other prominent members included John Skirrow Wright, an ardent reformer and Liberal councillor, and George Dixon. A recently-elected councillor, Dixon was passionately concerned with opening up education to children of all classes and would become a Birmingham MP recalled in a school named after him.

Dixon and his brother donated £1,000 to a new fund; as did Thomas Lloyd, George Frederick Muntz, and Louisa Anne Ryland, the heiress of the wide Ryland estates. Several other leading men gave between £100 and £500 so that a total of £7,000 was raised. This sum was added to that which the Company had already paid towards the purchase, and was offered to the Town Council if they would complete the undertaking. Langford wearily wrote that 'after several long and weary discussions', on February 2, 1864 the Council finally voted £20,000 for that purpose.

The Company's last meeting was held in May, when a testimonial was presented to Langford, in recognition of his services as honorary secretary. This consisted of 'a handsome gold watch, a copy of Knight's *Pictorial Shakespeare* in seven volumes, and Robert Bell's *Golden Leaves*'. The Company was then wound up and the purchase was completed by the Council on September 12, 1864. Ten days later Aston Park was at last opened as a Free Park by the Mayor, W. Holiday, who gave a banquet in the Great Gallery of Aston Hall in celebration.

The next day the *'Birmingham Daily Post'* reported that the Aston Hall and Park movement had been brought to a successful conclusion. For the previous seven

Children splashing in the paddling pool on a summer's day in the 1960s.

years it had been one of the prominent items of local agitations 'but its rate of progression has become more and more feeble with each succeeding year'. After the great fêtes of 1856, 'the whole community seemed animated with the sentiment "Save Aston Hall". A perfect whirlwind of enthusiasm then arose in favour of securing the old mansion and its appurtenances for public use'.

Importantly the newspaper maintained that 'the pioneers of the cause were a body of working men'. Their vital efforts were soon to be forgotten, as was the working-class campaign for public parks that had begun in the early 1850s. Langford himself wrote with some sorrow that:

> although the names of the donors of the £7,000 are very properly exhibited on a tablet in the entrance hall, no allusion is made to the working-men who gave up their shares, or to the company who had paid £14,000 towards the purchase of the Hall and Park, and who expended a large sum in beautifying the park, and collected at considerable cost, aided by donations, the exhibition which is now one of the chief attractions of the place. The shareholders generously gave all this to the town, and up to this time have received no word of recognition or of thanks for their act. Let us hope that impartial history will reverse this injustice, and render honour to whom honour is due.

The time to do so is well overdue.

Chapter 5

A Benefactor's Gifts: Cannon Hill Park and Small Heath Park

It is one of the most poignant stories in the history of Birmingham, of how the heart of Louisa Anne Ryland supposedly was broken by her father who forbade her to marry the man whom she loved. As privileged as she was, in a Victorian era in which the paternal word was as law, Louisa Anne was unable to defy her parents. The only child of Samuel Ryland and Anne Pemberton, she belonged to two of the most prominent and wealthy families in the town.

The Pembertons were mentioned as goldsmiths as far back as the later 1500s. In the succeeding generations some of them became ironmongers and money lenders – and with their riches from business they became significant landowners locally. Louisa Anne's paternal family was also embedded firmly within Birmingham. Her

A rare set of three photographs from the early twentieth century that show gardeners working on Cannon Hill Park. A plough team.

Rolling the grass.

A gardener at work.

The Edgbaston Road entrance to Cannon Hill Park decorated for the Coronation of Edward VI in 1901. Five years previously, Sir John Holder, the wealthy brewer, had given seven acres to add to the park; then in 1906 it was extended by almost three acres. This area was used as nursery gardens for the supply of plants to all Birmingham's parks; and interestingly since 1887 a garden had been especially adapted at the Park for students of botany. By the time of the Coronation the popularity of the park had been increased by tramway improvements which made it easily accessible from the city centre. Consequently many improvements were made including a tea-garden, an arboretum, and a new entrance from Russell Road.

grandfather, John, had a wire-drawing business and amassed a considerable fortune, which was increased by his marriage to Martha Ruston, a wealthy heiress whose family was important in the area from the late 1600s.

John and Martha Ryland were the grandparents of Louisa Anne. She was born in 1814 at the Laurels, Edgbaston. When their daughter was still but young, the Rylands moved from Birmingham to The Priory at Warwick. A few years later, when the railway cut through the estate, the Rylands settled at Barford Hill House in Sherbourne, which lay south of the county town. Like so many sons of those who had gained their money through the making of things, Samuel was set upon forgetting his origins. He wished instead to become a country gentleman.

To this end it is said that he determined that his daughter would marry into an aristocratic family, perhaps even that of the Lord Brooke, the owner of Warwick

The Parks Police in front of the South African War Memorial in August 1912. Designed by Albert Toft and unveiled in 1905, the Memorial is a bronze sculpture on a red granite pedestal. It is inscribed 'To the glorious memory of the SONS OF BIRMINGHAM who fell in South Africa 1899-1902 and to perpetuate the example of all who served in the Boer War. This memorial is erected by their fellow citizens'.

Women workers from the BSA at a 'Win the War Day' at Cannon Hill Park on September 21, 1918.

Castle. But Louisa Anne would have nothing of her father's plans. She had met and fallen in love with Henry Smith. He was the son of a leading brass founder and street commissioner, one of those who ran Birmingham before there was a town council from 1838 – and he himself would later become a councillor and Mayor. For all these connections, the young man was regarded as an unsuitable suitor for the hand of Samuel Ryland's daughter. Forbidden from marrying the one she had chosen, it was said that Louisa Anne Ryland resolved never to wed. Nor did she.

Louise Anne Ryland stayed with her parents and upon her father's death in 1843 she inherited great wealth. Aged 29 she owned extensive estates in Stratford and Sherbourne, and also in and around Birmingham. Blessed with riches, she could well have become an absentee landowner interested only in her enormous income from rents. She did not do so. As if she were rejecting her family's flight from Birmingham, Louisa Anne proceeded to shower gifts upon the town of her birth.

Owning much of Ladywood, she gave the land on which the church of Saint Barnabas was erected in the aptly named Ryland Street. This was backed up by a sum towards the building costs and on August 1, 1859, Louisa Anne laid the foundation stone for the new place of worship. Eight years later she set up the

Birmingham and Warwickshire fund to support six boys in the Wolverhampton Orphan Asylum, and in what was seen as 'an unparalleled act of munificence', she contributed £10,000 toward church building in Brum.

This exceptional gesture was surpassed in 1873 when the good-hearted heiress handed to the Council the freehold of over 66 acres of meadow land and dairy farm in Moseley to be used as a free park. It was estimated the value of the gift was about £25,000. Stretching along the banks of the Rea, the property had been bought by the Rylands in two lots. In 1788 Cannon Hill House, now the National Centre for Conductive Education, and its grounds had been purchased from Samuel Ruston; and then, in 1803, what was called the Horse Moors had been bought from William Jones Calcott.

The area needed attention before it was suitable for the visit of a large number of people so Louisa Anne paid £5,000 for it to be drained, laid out and planted. John Thackray Bunce declared that the result was impressive. The park boasted ornamental gardening; shrubberies that included rare evergreens; large pools surrounded by walks; a carriage drive; a refreshment room and entrance house; a boat house; a bathing pool; and a set of dressing rooms.

Located to the south-west in what was then Worcestershire countryside, Cannon Hill Park was upwind and away from the smoke and smells of central and east Birmingham. Two miles distant from the town it was but a 30 minute walk away.

Playing cricket during the 1920s. In the background is the 'Golden Lion'. Once located on Deritend High Street, this had been dismantled, moved and then re-erected in the Park in 1911 because of road widening. The work was funded by the Birmingham and Warwickshire Archaeological Society. The building was used as a cricket pavilion until the early 1980s.

Swimming at Cannon Hill Park during the inter-war years; a photograph taken by F. R. Logan. Initially both the open-air bathing and boating pool were leased out; then in 1899 the Baths and Parks Department took control of the bathing pool. The Council made bathing free here and at Small Heath Park on Saturdays and Wednesday afternoons. Both open-air swimming baths were closed in 1938 because of declining attendances and the cost of making them fit for Ministry of Health standards.

This made the park accessible, healthy and pleasant, according to the *'Birmingham Daily Post'* – and its position in a river valley afforded it a 'picturesque view' of 'the higher portions of the town', which stood out in bold relief.

The report commended the work of the park's designer, Mr J. Gibson of Battersea. He had taken advantage of all the natural characteristics of the ground, including its undulating nature and old trees, and 'supplemented them in the best possible taste with work that is at once novel and consistent with them'. The park's charming appearance was enhanced by rivulets, and newly-planted shrubberies, flower beds, well-kept lawns and pools. Swans, ducks and other ornamental aquatic birds were to be introduced to the pools, which already abounded with water lilies and similar plants.

Adding to the park's appeal was a large open space 'where visitors can do pretty much as they please, where the youngsters can play their cricket or trap ball, and many other games in which the youthful mind is prone to delight'. There was also a railed off children's playground, which was described 'as a very wise provision if adhered to strictly in as much as the children will be in nobody's way, and nobody will be in theirs'.

In the upper north-west of the park was 'a charming and delightful retreat' called a fernery – where 'an admirable piece of landscaping may be seen'. As for the bathing pool, it was in the course of construction. It was to be 216 feet by 110 feet in size and to have a depth between 2.5 and 3 feet. Boasting 'an excellent concrete bottom', the pool was to be supplied with 'water from springs, and other sources and will be kept fresh and pure'. It was also to be sheltered by a newly-planted ring of trees and shrubs, whilst dressing booths were available for bathers.

There were plans for hothouses for plants and seating to be placed around the park. As the *'Birmingham Daily Post'* announced, 'there is yet much to be done before the place is anything like complete; but when a few years are over, and the shrubs and trees begin to grow, the people of Birmingham will have great reason to be proud of this, the latest addition to their public parks'.

So they would do and on the day of its opening on September 1, 1873 it was estimated that 15,000 people visited Cannon Hill Park. Modestly, Louisa Anne

The staff of Cannon Hill Park in 1937, with the green houses in the background – these are now gone. Thanks to Jim Winn whose brother, Arthur, is on the left of the front row.

Ryland had turned down the suggestion that the park should be called after herself, although she attended the opening. Before the gates were officially unlocked, the Mayor, Ambrose Biggs, called for three hearty cheers for her, which was 'enthusiastically responded to'. She was cheered as loudly and heartily when she left.

Each person who visited the Park that day was given a card inscribed with this comment by Louisa Anne:

> Through the bounty of God, I have great pleasure in giving Cannon Hill Park to the Corporation of Birmingham for the use of the people of the town and neighbourhood. I would express my earnest hope that the park may prove a source of healthful recreation to the people of Birmingham, and that they will aid in the protection and preservation of what is now their own property.

Louisa Anne Ryland was one of the most substantial benefactors in Birmingham's history. Amongst her mighty gifts were donations of £10,000 each towards the School of Art in Edmund Street and the Birmingham and Midland Institute, and also 41 acres of land in Small Heath for another park. Formerly a farm and with a frontage to the Coventry road, this site was given in June 1876. Because it had been agricultural land it was costly to adapt to 'an ornamental use'.

Two lads in Small Heath Park in the early 1900s.

Children on the swing boats at Small Heath Park at the turn of the twentieth century.

As Bunce noted, the £10,000 estimate prepared by the Baths and Parks Committee for this purpose 'excited some unfavourable comment, whereupon Miss Ryland, having approved of the plans, signified her wish to contribute £4,000 towards the outlay'. A few days before the opening of Small Heath Park on April 5, 1879, the *'Birmingham Daily Post'* reported that it possessed a refreshment room and 'a capital boating pool' with two islands, a bridge and water fowl that was filled from a bore hole in the park.

The work on the park had been carried out under the joint supervision of the Borough Surveyor, Mr M. S. Till, and the Superintendent of Parks, Mr A. Rodway. Overall the grounds had been laid out and planted with great care, in connection with which Mr Hearn, the park keeper at Cannon Hill, had rendered great assistance. Moreover local contractors had played an important role. The lodge, refreshment room and bridge were built by John Dowse of Victoria Street, Small Heath; the

This photo was taken by the late Harold Wareham on November 1st, 1972. It shows Small Heath Park a few days before Bonfire Night. The fair is set up, whilst the bonfire itself – topped by a huge Guy – is also ready. 'Bonfires & Fireworks Carnivals' were held there from 1961 with thousands attending. They also took place at Senneleys Park, Summerfield Park and Pype Hayes Park and these great municipal bonfires were put on to reduce 'the number of back-garden bonfires, and this change in pattern could mean a decrease in the number of accidents caused by the inexperienced use of fireworks'.

carriage drives and pathways were laid out by Messrs Currall and Lewis of Icknield Port Road; and the iron fencing was erected by John Elwell of Sheepcote Street.

On the day of the opening, some local people hung out flags from their windows to show 'their appreciation of Miss Ryland's generosity'. A procession was formed at the corner of Cattell Road and Herbert Road. It was headed by the Hay Mills Band and included members of the local Foresters and Oddfellows friendly societies as well as of the Small Heath Literary and Scientific Society. They escorted the Mayor, Alderman Jesse Collings, to the Park where thousands of people had assembled despite the heavy rain to hear speeches and the Police Band

Four years later, an open-air bathing pool was added to the Park's facilities, followed by a bandstand in 1887. That year on Wednesday March 23, Queen Victoria visited Birmingham. It was the year of her Golden Jubilee and she came to lay the foundation stone of the Law Courts in Corporation Street. The day was observed as a Bank Holiday and there was great rejoicing at the Queen's arrival.

She alighted at Small Heath and Sparkbrook Railway Station at 1.15 pm. After a salute by the 1st Worcestershire Artillery Volunteers of Balsall Heath she and her party were escorted in their carriages via a new road laid out by the BSA across its land. Several thousand workers and members of the families cheered her as she was taken thence up to Golden Hillock Road. This was lined with happy school children and local folk who had paid to stand on buses, milk floats and farm wagons.

The Queen was then taken into Small Heath Park from its Wordsworth Road entrance, where a beautiful floral arch had been erected. The *'York Herald'* announced that the Park was filled with fifteen thousand schoolchildren, although later estimates stated 40-50,000. Be that as it may, they were in a fever of anxiety to see the Queen, whilst 'Her Majesty seemed equally delighted to see them. She and Princess Beatrice responded with the sweetest of smiles and bows to the shrill cheers which their appearance provoked'.

It had been intended that the children would sing the National Anthem 'but in their excitement this was forgotten. They could do nothing but shout and wave their handkerchiefs and capes with juvenile vehemence'. After the Queen left for the city centre, the youngsters were given buns courtesy of the Parks Department. To commemorate her visit the Mayor requested her Majesty's permission to change the name of Small Heath Park to Victoria Park. This was granted, although local people have continued to call it by its original name.

Chapter 6

Lungs for a Great City: Highgate Park and Summerfield Park

At the opening of Cannon Hill Park, the Mayor had asserted that 'the people are the guardians of their own park'. This was something that working-class campaigners for free parks had been agitating for since at least the early 1850s. The report of the event in the *'Birmingham Daily Post'* on September 3, 1873 also affirmed that 'the great need for vacant spaces where the working population of Birmingham can enjoy pure air and find the means of recreation is so well recognised as to require no demonstration'.

This statement signified that the argument for the provision of public parks was no longer contentious. After 40 years, the views of Alderman Cutler, Charles Bowyer Adderley, Joseph Sturge, George Dawson, John Alfred Langford, Daniel O'Neill and many others were now accepted. And the people of Birmingham had shown that they greatly appreciated the parks that had been provided for them. In 1871 the numbers of visitors at Calthorpe Park had been 40,610; at Adderley Park, 15,600; and at Aston Park, 127,370. This gave a total of 183,580.

Birmingham's citizens were soon to have more public parks to enjoy and henceforth the Council itself would become more important in their provision than would be benefactors. This shift to municipal action was reflected in a wider change in attitude as to the responsibilities of the Council to its citizens. Once notorious for its indecisiveness and penny-pinching, Birmingham's Council would soon be praised by an American journalist called Julian Ralph as 'the best governed city in the world' (*'Harper's New Monthly Magazine'*, 81, June, 1890). This amazing transformation was the long-term result of the preachings of ministers like George Dawson and the short-term dynamism of Joseph Chamberlain.

If Matthew Boulton bestrides the history of Birmingham in the eighteenth century, then Joseph Chamberlain spans the nineteenth century. Supported actively by a band of Liberal (later Liberal Unionist) politicians and by the majority of the people of the city, Chamberlain's energy coursed through a Birmingham that he was instrumental in changing for the better.

He was born in 1836 in London, a connection brought to mind by his home called Highbury and the adjacent Highbury Park in Moseley. Chamberlain was a

Children at Highgate Park in the early 1900s. A few years later, the fountain which had stood for many years in the centre of the Market Hall was moved to Highgate Park. This had been designed and manufactured by the famed firm of Messenger's on Broad Street, which had occupied part of what is now Centenary Square. Makers of 'chandeliers, candelabras, tripods, lamps and lanterns of every description, and other ornamental works in bronze and ormolu, also brass founders', they had been acclaimed at the Great Exhibition of 1851. That same year their 'handsome fountain of bronze' was erected in the centre of the Market Hall. It was adorned with well-designed figures representing the various market trades such as fish, fruit, and flowers. The fountain was moved because it became an obstruction.

teenager when he arrived in Birmingham to keep an eye on his father's large investment in the screw-making firm of John Nettlefold. The Nettlefolds were close relations to the Chamberlains and young Joseph soon took over the commercial and financial side of the business. He proved himself to be most successful and by the 1870s, Nettlefold and Chamberlain was one of the biggest concerns in the locality. With premises at Broad Street and Heath Street in Smethwick it employed more than 2,500 workers.

As a Unitarian, someone who did not believe in the Trinity of God the Father, God the Son and God the Holy Ghost, Chamberlain was motivated not only by a

Children playing at Highgate Park in the 1930s - with the old Rowton House, now the Chamberlain Hotel, in Alcester Street in the background.

desire to do well and to make money but also to work on behalf of others less fortunate. He worshipped at the Church of the Messiah on Broad Street. From 1869, the minister there was Henry William Crosskey. A Liberal Party activist, Crosskey was a key figure in the development of women's rights organisations in Birmingham and a proponent of the Civic Gospel.

In 1876 he wrote that Birmingham was characterised by two things. First, 'the individual interest felt in the just government of the town and the nation'; and second 'the widespread conviction that a just government means a government under which not only the conditions of physical health and prosperity should be secured but opportunities for receiving the largest culture and enjoying the best results of science and are brought by corporate action within the reach of the greatest possible number' (Henry Crosskey, 'The "600" of Birmingham', *'Macmillan's Magazine'*, 35, November 1876 – April 1877).

Of course corporate action was something that Dawson had been struggling for since at least the 1850s; so too had his successor at the Baptist Mount Zion, Charles Vince; and so too had Robert William Dale, the pastor of Carrs Lane Congregationalist church since 1854. Dale believed intensely that politics was a high calling, damning those who refused to use their political power as 'guilty of treachery both to God and men'.

In his book *'The Laws of Christ for Common Life'* (1884) he avowed that municipalities could do more for the people than Parliament. They could diminish the amount of sickness in the community and prolong life and thus save thousands of children from becoming orphans; they could improve miserable homes which were fatal to health; and 'they can give to the poor the enjoyment of pleasant parks and gardens, and the intellectual cultivation and refinement of public libraries and galleries of art'.

For many years the voices of Dale and Dawson had fallen on barren ground. Then, as Dale recounted, towards the end of the 1860s 'a few Birmingham men made the discovery that perhaps a strong and able Town Council might do almost as much to improve the conditions of life of the town as parliament itself'. This discovery would soon 'invest the Council with a new attractiveness and dignity'. So it did.

The most significant man to heed the call of the Civic Gospel was Joseph Chamberlain. He joined others at the Unitarian Church of the Messiah on Broad Street in teaching working men who wished to improve their education on Sundays and

A woman looks at the flowers by the statue of Edward VII in Highgate Park in the 1950s. Unveiled in 1913 in Victoria Square, it was moved to Highgate Park in 1951 when Victoria Square was remodelled. It has now been returned to its original site.

weekday evenings. A passionate believer in opening up education to everyone, in 1867 and along with George Dixon and other leading Liberals, he launched the Birmingham Educational Society. It later merged with the National Education League and pushed for state funding for schools and a non-sectarian education. The campaign was partially successful when the Elementary Education Act was passed in 1870.

Increasingly drawn to political action, in 1869 Chamberlain was elected to the town council. Within a short time his dynamism had gathered about him a band of sympathetic councillors. Many of them were also wealthy Unitarians who were inter-related. They included the Byngs, Kenricks and Martineaus. With an influx of younger and more committed councillors, Chamberlain was able to take control of the Council as Mayor in 1873. Under him this was no honorary office, rather it enabled him to act decisively for the good of Birmingham.

He held office for three years and his impact was amazing. He forced through building bye-laws which effectively forbade the further building of back-to-back houses; he thrust forward sewerage and drainage schemes to make the town healthier; and he secured the passage of acts which allowed the Corporation to take over the private gas and water companies, thus bringing light and fresh water to the furthest courtyard.

More than this, he oversaw the bringing in of a Health Committee on the Council to supervise and improve the public health of the town; he watched over the setting up of a municipal fire brigade; he encouraged the building of the Council

Joseph Chamberlain standing in the car at Summerfield Park on his triumphal tour of Birmingham on his 70th birthday in July 1906.

A flower bed in Summerfield Park in 1911 declaring 'Long Live Our King and Queen', for the Coronation of King George VI.

House; he campaigned for the cutting of Corporation Street; and he authorised the writing of the *'History of the Corporation of Birmingham'*.

This programme of municipal socialism was led by a capitalist and entrepreneur, but Chamberlain realised that in a large urban centre, the local authority had a duty to own the utilities that were essential for the health and happiness of the citizens in general. Importantly, his municipal activity was profitable. Elected as an MP in 1876 for Birmingham West, Chamberlain continued to hold dear the city of his adoption and he was largely responsible for the creation of The University of Birmingham in 1900.

It was also under Chamberlain's mayoralty that Birmingham gained its first truly municipal park, in that its purchase was both sought and paid for solely by the Council. This was Highgate Park. About eight acres in size, it was situated on the slope leading down from the Moseley Road to Alcester Street and was enclosed by these two streets and by the backs of houses and factories in Darwin Street and Moseley Street.

The site had been an enclosed pasture belonging to an Elizabeth Hollier but in her will of 1790, she had left it in trust. The income from the property was to be used to buy coats, gowns and shifts for twelve or more poor men and women of Birmingham and eight or more of Aston. From 1862, there had been appeals by public bodies that the charity's land should be used for a park and eight years later discussions began in earnest. There were several motives for the Council's interest.

At its January 1870 meeting Councillor Simmons supported moves to buy the land as 'in its present state it was the report of all the roughs of the neighbourhood, especially on Sundays'. He articulated a widespread fear of the gathering of gangs of large numbers of 'rough' young men and teenaged boys for gambling and fighting in places away from the watchful eye of the police. Most especially it was feared that such gatherings could lead to disorder on the streets and threaten respectable members of society.

Councillor Simmons also felt that the land was 'in a densely populated neighbourhood and would be very valuable as a recreation ground'. Another supporter of the purchase was Alderman Henry Hawkes. Back in 1853 and as Mayor he had presided over the meeting held at the Public Office 'to take into consideration a project providing a public park for the inhabitants of the town'. Now Hawkes rejoiced that the people of 'Bordesley and Deritend were at last to get something out of the rates' as he did not think that they had enjoyed their share hitherto.

Negotiations for the land were protracted but on May 25, 1875, the Council paid the charity £8,100 for its purchase. By now the fences which had surrounded the pasture had come down and as the *'Birmingham Post'* described on April 26, 1876 'unfenced and uncared for it soon became a perfect wilderness, covered in litter, dusty in summer, muddy in winter and, altogether an eyesore to all who saw it'. Now with hard work, thought and £4,500 it was in the throes of transformation.

The Band of the Scots Guards at Summerfield Park just before the First World War.

Mr Cresswell of Five Ways put up the lodge, fences, and gate; whilst Mr Coudrey, the nurseryman and landscape gardener of Ampton Road, laid it out. Their work was supervised by the Baths and Parks Committee of the Council and Mr Rodway, the parks superintendent. The local newspaper was delighted that under Mr Coudrey's hands 'the desert is rapidly being converted into a paradise'. He divided it into two main portions by way of a terrace ten yards wide. Plane trees were planted nine yards in from each side of the terrace so that 'in a few years it will provide a pleasant grove'.

In the centre of the park a flight of steps led to a broad gravel path which 'diverges right and left around a large plot of grass, nearly circular in form and about 80 yards in diameter'. On the other side of the paths, raised beds were filled with a large variety of evergreen and flowering shrubs. Below the grass plot was a children's playground 100 yards by 60 yards in extent. This was to be laid with tar asphalt so as to be dry and clean. Indeed the park had a twofold purpose as a children's playground and promenade, as opposed to nearby Calthorpe Park which was popular with sportsmen especially cricketers.

All around the park were 'tastefully arranged beds filled with shrubs, which after a year or two's growth will shut out the view to the back premises of the adjoining properties'. Trees had been planted plentifully alongside the footpaths 'to give an abundance of shade'. Above the terrace, the park had been laid out in plots of grass and shrubbery beds 'divided by pleasantly winding paths'. Chestnuts, ashes, laburnums, limes and other trees had been 'so disposed as to give the ground as much as possible the appearance of a garden'. Water pipes were laid throughout. At frequent intervals along them were hydrants so that the park's 'greenness may be preserved by frequent watering in the dry season'.

The reporter for the *'Birmingham Daily Post'* stressed that Highgate Park would 'form a breathing space for a heavily populated district'. So it would for Highgate was densely packed with factories, workshops and back-to-backs. Located as it was on the red sandstone ridge above the River Rea, the park also provided 'probably the best view of the southern prospect of Birmingham' – from the green and pleasant suburb of Edgbaston to the forest of chimneys of all shapes and sizes and church spires of Birmingham.

Here in Highgate Park 'the labour-wearied artisan and other inhabitants of the town will be able to survey the scene of their daily toil at a distance where they might find it interesting without being troublesome, and here, in a little "oasis" as it were in the desert, they will be able to obtain the recreation they need'.

Originally it was intended to call the new facility Camp Hill Park, but this idea was abandoned as the name was supposed to bear too close a resemblance to Cannon Hill Park and so might lead to confusion. Thus Highgate Park was opened by the Mayor, Joseph Chamberlain, on June 2, 1876 – the same day as Louisa Anne Ryland gifted

Small Heath Park to the City. Dent waxed lyrical that 'no-one who had aforetime crossed the dismal piece of land, crowded with brick-ends and other unsightly refuse – the once pleasant greensward worn bare and brown – would have readily identified it with the exquisite little park, with its broad terrace and winding walks, its shrubberies and bright parterres, and its smooth trim lawns, as it appeared after the transformation'.

As for the Mayor, Alderman Chamberlain, he received the keys for the park and with pleasure opened 'that new garden for its people, and that new playground for their children'. Chamberlain stated that the provision of parks had occupied the attention of the Council for many years, and he highlighted Alderman Cutler's efforts in this field. In keeping with his fervent belief in the importance of local government and in tune with local antagonism towards London, Chamberlain blamed the failure to provide parks on the lack of funding from national government.

Ignoring the dismal and damaging dominance of the Economists and the general absence of Council support for Adderley's plans and the working-men's campaign for free parks, Chamberlain pronounced that Government bodies 'invariably replied that they had no money for the provinces'. With a distinctive interpretation at odds with the evidence, he declared that 'what the Government had refused to do for us the munificence of some of our citizens and the energy of the Town Council had provided for ourselves'.

He was right about the role of benefactors but greatly exaggerated the role of a Council that had been admonished by Queen Victoria into buying Aston Park. Of course, Chamberlain was then standing for election to Parliament and attacks on London-centric national governments always played well in Birmingham. As it was a few days later he was returned unopposed as MP for West Birmingham.

In his speech at Highgate Park, Chamberlain stressed that he did not need to dwell on the necessity of open spaces 'the importance of having these lungs for great cities, breathing places for their toiling and industrious population'. That he did not need to do so was thanks to the resolute and undaunted campaigning of philanthropists like Adderley, preachers such as Dawson, and working men of the ilk of Langford and O'Neill. The argument for public parks had indeed been won, but as Chamberlain made plain, quick action was still needed.

He explained that Birmingham's population had more than doubled in a generation. Many who were still alive recalled 'places which now were covered with a wilderness of small houses and smoky chimneys as green fields, pleasant sward to walk upon, and pleasant sights to see'. Unfortunately, the rise in population had been accompanied by an increase in the value of land that made it 'impossible for ordinary working men to have gardens attached to their dwellings'. Most had to be content with only a yard to look upon, even if it were chiefly occupied by a washhouse and ashpit. Useful as these were 'they were not very beautiful to look upon, and not very conducive to health'.

The famed jazz musician, Andy Hamilton, performing with his band 'The Blue Notes' at a jazz festival at Summerfield Park in the late 1960s. Andy is on the saxophone and his great friend, the late Ron Daley, known musically as Sam Brown, is on the piano.

Under such circumstances, Chamberlain was certain that 'no time was to be lost if they were to provide for the whole population of Birmingham places for recreation and innocent enjoyment within easy reach, if they were to provide for the residents of Birmingham such places as Highgate Park'. He hoped that leading citizens desired 'to keep alive in the hearts and minds of the people some sense of beauty – then the provision of trees with green foliage, of shrubs and of beautiful flowers, was as necessary to their elevation as schools, and libraries, and galleries of art'.

Chamberlain affirmed that 'it was simple nonsense to wonder at the intemperate habits of some portion of their population, or to complain about their roughness of manners, if they did not provide some better opportunities for innocent enjoyment; if they did give them greater scope for the cultivation of taste and refinement than the necessary conditions of their dwellings provided'. He thought it was a misfortune that in great manufacturing cities, the dedication to the practical business and work of life made people forget 'the ugliness of ordinary English existence, and the dull uniformity which distinguished it'.

This ugliness and uniformity had a bad influence for all of them. In Chamberlain's mind beautiful buildings, fine statues and pleasant gardens 'were as much a power in the education of the people as any other to which they devoted attention'. These things 'the rich were able to provide for themselves, but it was the duty of the Town Council as representing and caring for all the community, to provide similar advantages for all, and to make all partakers in the enjoyments which otherwise would be confined to a few'. The Mayor then declared the park open for the people of Birmingham, and in so doing he 'confided it to the care of the people as their property and for their benefit'.

Clearly, Chamberlain's words were deeply influenced by the Civic Gospel of Dawson, Dale and Crosskey and by his own experiences and beliefs. They were also affected by his political awareness. Many skilled and semi-skilled working-class men had been able to vote since 1867. Working-class support and votes were vital to Chamberlain's local prominence and national ambitions. Through an innovative and dynamic policy of municipal socialism that had seen the takeover by the Council of the private water and gas companies, he had ensured popular support for his policies and for the Liberal Party of which he was a leading member.

Chamberlain went on to become a major player on the national stage, but his bedrock was Birmingham and he continued to be fervently backed by the working-class of the town. They followed him whatever his decision. When he broke with Gladstone and the Liberals in 1886 over the issue of Home Rule for Ireland, they backed him as he established the Liberal Unionist party and allied himself with the Conservatives. And they followed him again in 1906 when he split the Conservatives over his support for the imposition of tariffs on foreign goods. They did so because of his passion for Birmingham and his policy of municipal socialism.

The provision of parks had been a crucial aspect of Chamberlain's programme of municipalisation and of the creation of the 'best-governed city in the world, a city worthy of comparison with renaissance Florence, Milan and Venice'. Succeeding generations of councillors would uphold Chamberlain's belief that the Council should represent and care for all the community, and provide similar advantages for all. The period of true municipal parks began with Highgate Park and on June 6, 1876, within four days of its opening, the Council purchased land for its second park on its own initiative.

This was the Summerfield House and Estate between the Dudley Road and Icknield Port Road in Winson Green. Formerly the home of the late Lucas Chance of the famed glassmaking firm of Smethwick, it covered about twelve acres and was bought for £9,000. Another £3,500 was spent on laying out Summerfield Park. It was opened soon afterwards, on July 29, by the Mayor, Alderman Baker, who had recently been elected to the mayoralty after Joseph Chamberlain's election as MP.

Over the next few years, Summerfield Park was enlarged twice by about 21 acres in total. In Dent's opinion, these extensions enabled the Parks Committee 'to considerably improve and increase the ornamental portion of the park, by transferring the site for cricket, football, etc., to the newly acquired land'.

Summerfield House was demolished during this period and a band stand was erected on its site.

In 1906, Summerfield Park was one of those visited by Joseph Chamberlain on his triumphal tour of Birmingham to celebrate his 70th birthday. The celebrations began at 3.30 pm on the afternoon of Saturday July 7 with a motor car procession that left Victoria Square. Fittingly Chamberlain was carried in a Birmingham-made Lanchester. Within ten minutes the parade had reached Victoria Park, Small Heath and by 6.20 pm it had also gone slowly through Ward End Park, Aston Park, Victoria Park, Handsworth, Summerfield Park and Calthorpe Park. At each of them Chamberlain received an address and then spoke to the great crowds that had gathered.

That afternoon and evening Victoria Park, Small Heath was the venue for entertainment with music, song, jugglers, Punch and Judy and humorous selections whilst the Small Heath Harriers Swimming Club gave an aquatic display in the pool. Children from the council schools at Allcock Street, Floodgate Street and Somerville Road also put on an exhibition of drill, marching and maypole dancing, after which the Birmingham City Prize band played. The evening was finished with

Children playing in Chamberlain Gardens in the 1970s.

A family outing at Perry Park in 1928. Thanks to Mrs I. Wagstaff.

a fireworks display. Similar festivities were held at the other parks in which Chamberlain had been feted.

He died in 1914 and eight years later Chamberlain Gardens were opened in his memory. An area of five acres in Edgbaston, it was gifted for this purpose by Mr and the Honourable Mrs Anstruther Gough-Calthorpe; whilst a grant from the Feeney Trustees was made to the laying out of the land.

The previous year, 1913, the Perry Reservoir had been transferred by Birmingham's Water Committee to the Parks Committee and was opened as a boating pool. Soon after, the Council authorised a loan of £7,053 for the purchase of about 87 acres of land surrounding the reservoir. Twenty acres were let at a rental to the Estates Department for the purpose of allotments, and the remainder became Perry Park. Vince explained that 'the expense of laying-out was inconsiderable, the land being naturally adapted for the purpose. It was hoped that the park would be used not only by the adjoining suburbs but by the townspeople, who could reach it by a short walk from the terminus of the Perry Barr tramway'. Water and parks are a fitting memory to Chamberlain, the politician who transformed Birmingham and thrust its Council on to the world stage.

Chapter 7

The Duty to do Good: Recreation Grounds

Writing in 1878 in the first volume of the *'History of the Corporation of Birmingham'*, J. T. Bunce compared the contemporary condition of the town glowingly with that of 40 years previously, when the Council had first begun its work. With a confidence and pride buoyed by the successes of Joseph Chamberlain's recent mayoralty, he asserted that the government of the town was in 'its own hands, free, unfettered, and complete'. Birmingham now had public edifices worthy of its status; the streets were well kept, lighted, drained, and watched; and it possessed the administration of justice by its own magistrates and courts.

The private monopolies of gas and water had ceased and their undertakings had passed into the hands of the community; whilst the health of the population was cared for by an efficient system of sanitary measures and its cleanliness by way of baths and wash-houses. Opportunities of culture were offered to all classes through free libraries and museums of art, and recreation was now provided by parks and pleasure-grounds, some of them the gifts of public benefactors.

It had taken years of struggle to achieve these benefits of corporate government for the people, but Bunce was justified with his praise. In the battle for municipal action, the working-class campaign for public parks free to the people had played a significant role – one which sadly was to be lost sight of. By contrast the role of benefactors was never forgotten. Nonetheless by the 1870s the principle of public parks had been not only embraced but also acted upon.

Thereafter the importance of public parks was never questioned in Birmingham. In 1902, Charles Vince, the author of the third volume of the *'History of the Corporation'*, observed that although the history of the Baths Department from 1885 could hardly be called progress, by contrast the Parks Department moved forward and suffered no rebuffs. Indeed far from its councillors finding 'their zeal for extension checked by the thrift of the Council they never failed to carry without dissent all their proposals for enlarging or improving the parks'.

On two occasions the Council had actually insisted upon projects which the Baths and Park Committee had declined to recommend upon financial grounds. As Vince commented, 'the building of baths may at any time be deferred to a more convenient season; but opportunities of preserving open spaces must be taken at once or they may be lost for ever'. The opening of Small Heath Park in 1876 had brought the total of parks owned by Birmingham to seven. More would soon follow but increasingly the attention of councillors was also drawn to the real need to provide smaller recreation grounds within the heavily-built up, polluted and overcrowded central wards of the town.

An impetus to this movement was given in 1877 by William Middlemore, who presented to the Corporation about four acres of land in Burbury Street, Hockley, on the boundary with Aston Manor. He was a descendant of the ancient and staunchly Catholic family of Middlemores of Edgbaston and Hazelwell and had become wealthy through his success with his saddlery and leather business. Radical in politics, Middlemore was elected a town councillor and became one of the founders of the Birmingham Liberal Association in 1865 and of the Education League four years later.

His own immediate ancestors had ceased to be Catholics and became Anglicans, but William himself was a Baptist. He gave generously to the building of Baptist chapels, but with his brothers Richard and James also rebuilt the chancel of Edgbaston Parish Church. As for the land he donated in Burbury Street, he paid for its laying out. This included trees and parterres of flowers and trees; paving with asphalt; and fencing. The total cost was estimated at £12,000.

Children playing at the Burbury Street Recreation Ground in the 1950s. Playing at recreation grounds like these and at many parks was always referred to by young Brummies as 'going over the Rec'.

The Recreation Ground was formally opened on December, 1, 1877 by the Mayor, William Kenrick. A huge crowd of 10,000 people turned up. It included 6,000 children from the local schools who had marched to the ground. As they arrived each was given a bun paid for by William Middlemore. In his response to various speeches praising his generosity, he explained that 'if it was a pleasure for them to recognise that gift it was a luxury for him to make it. To do something for the town of his birth, which he loved and honoured so much was gratification indeed'.

Middlemore realised that the town's authorities were 'fully alive to the duty of providing for the improvement, comfort and recreation of the population, as was evidenced by the schools, free libraries, baths and parks that they had supplied'. He was delighted that this was a very different situation to that 50 years before and he felt proud 'that they had a Corporation worthy of its vocation' as well as public benefactors such as Sir Charles Adderley and 'that noble lady Miss Ryland, who had done so much for the benefit of the poorer classes'. Middlemore finished with a call to more townsmen to adopt the motto 'the great truth that the power to do good involved the duty to do it'.

The *'Birmingham Daily Post'* was certain that the Burbury Street Recreation Ground would be of great benefit 'as a playground for children and for the artisans of this densely-populated district'. So it proved to be – and more such places were to follow. In 1878, legislation empowered the Corporation to take over the town's disused churchyard and burial-grounds and to convert them into public gardens or recreation grounds, subject to the consent of the Bishop of Worcester and of the clergy of the respective parishes.

The first of these to be dealt with was the burial ground in Park Street that belonged to St. Martin's Parish. Dent declaimed its condition 'which had long been a scandal to the town, its walls broken, gravestones thrown down and destroyed, and the ground itself a wilderness covered with brick-ends and unsightly refuse of every description'. The ground was divided by Fazeley Street and was taken over by the Corporation in 1879. It was 'tastefully laid out with flower-beds, shrubs, and walks', and these Park Street Gardens were opened to the public by the Mayor, Richard Chamberlain, on June 25, 1880.

Just across Duddeston Row was St. Bartholomew's churchyard, which was laid out about the same time. Two years later year, in 1882, and after requests from local people, St Mary's graveyard in the Gun Quarter was transformed into a public recreation ground called St Mary's Gardens. Two others followed quickly. Following a memorial by residents in St Stephen's Ward, the Council acquired a 99 year lease from the Governors of King Edward's School of part of the 'Old Pleck', near Newtown Row.

This had been the location for the Onion Fair, after it had been moved out of the city centre and before it went on to the Serpentine at Aston. After the Council took control of the Old Pleck, just over an acre was laid out, paved with asphalt and opened as the Walmer Recreation Ground, on Saturday April 9, 1892. The *'Birmingham Daily Post'* gave credit to those who had induced the Corporation to secure this open space as a lung 'for the thousands of young people living in this crowded ward'.

Still it was a pity that it was so small, as 'in no locality is such a space more badly needed'. So it was. In 1909 and 1910 an investigation would be carried out into the very poor wards of St Stephen's and St George's. It divided the population according to the weekly income of the head of household. Where this was more than 20 shillings (£1) a week (about the poverty line for a moderately-sized family) the infant mortality rate was 140 per 1000 live births; but where it was less than this the rate rose alarmingly to 210. Furthermore babies born to the poorest section and who survived until twelve months old weighed on average a pound less than the babies belonging to the slightly better-off group.

The Council continued to take opportunities to provide playgrounds for children, as Vince put it in Volume 4 of the *'History of the Corporation'*, 'living in poor streets remote from the open fields and the larger municipal parks'. This policy was costly, 'though there were no indications that the expense was grudged by any section of the ratepayers'. In 1879 the Gas Committee had temporarily opened a piece of its land close to St Clements Road, Nechells as a recreation ground. Thirteen years later it was placed under the management of the Baths and Parks Committee. The Gas Committee spent £600 on improving the ground, and paid for its maintenance. It was, however, understood that it might be required at any time for the extension of the gas works.

By the end of the 1890s two other grounds had been opened. The first was St Mark's Recreation Ground in Ladywood, where the open spaces that remained were few and small; and the second was St Paul's Gardens in the Jewellery Quarter. This latter was described by Kathleen Dayus in *'Her People'* (1982), her compelling and moving account of growing up poor locally. In down-to-earth language that has no hint of self-pity or bitterness at the dire conditions she and her folk endured, she brings to the fore how important this space was.

No-one had a garden, not a blade of grass. There were cobblestones everywhere.

> If we wanted to see any flowers we went to the churchyard to play. We were often sent there, out of the way of our parents. We would take a bottle of tea and some milk for the younger ones who were transported in our go-cart. We nicknamed the churchyard 'Titty-bottle Park', a name that stuck with us for years. We'd tie the go-cart to a tree or a tombstone and play at hide and seek or perhaps some of us would change the stale water in the jam jars and rearrange the flowers. We'd be happy for a while playing at our games until the vicar appeared with his stick to chase us away. But try as he might he could never get rid of us; we always returned the next day.

In 1906, the Corporation acquired about two acres of land fronting Musgrave Road in Winson Green as a recreation ground. The Parks Committee had actually declined to purchase it as too expensive, but had been overruled by the full Council. As Vince stated, this incident marked the beginning of 'a resolute effort to provide all the poor children of the City with accessible playgrounds'. The next year the Birmingham Playgrounds, Open Spaces, and Playing Fields Society was formed under the chairmanship of John Nettlefold. Its aim was 'the purpose of discovering any opportunity that might befall of preserving an open space, and of stimulating the liberality both of landowners and private citizens and of the Council itself'.

The Society's efforts were not always welcomed by the Baths and Parks Committee but it exerted great influence on the Council as a whole, for Nettlefold was the chairman of the Housing Committee and a noted figure in the emerging field of town planning. All the Society's projects were adopted and thus, as Vince noted ironically, 'for the common experience of the zeal of a spending Committee held in check by the Council, was substituted the singular spectacle of a Council insisting on expenditure which the spending committee condemned as unnecessary or extravagant'.

Soon after the Society was formed, the Council accepted three open spaces from it. The first was six acres in Somerville Road, Small Heath, afterwards called Digby

Lawford Street Recreation Ground packed with children in 1928. Like many recreation grounds it disappeared in the post-war redevelopment of the central districts of Birmingham.

A mother and daughter and an old lady in a yard in Adams Street, close to the Oxygen Street that was described so vividly by the Reverend Bass. Notice the spotlessly white pinafores of the child and her mother – a woman, like so many amongst the poor, who strove valiantly to stay clean despite the pollution all around.

Park after its donor Mr C. W. Digby – whose family owned much of the area. As for the second, this was under an acre of land on Coventry Street, intended to be called the Gooch Recreation Grounds, again after the donor who was one of the biggest landowners in Birmingham. The third was another small plot in Tower Street, St George's Ward which became an asphalted playground. This was little used and sold in 1913. The money raised then paid for a large recreation ground on the other side of Tower Street.

Acting vigorously, in 1907 the Society, supported by 'many public-spirited Citizens', ensured that the Council took on three more small plots in Oxygen Street, Lawford Street in Vauxhall, and Communication Row on Holloway Head. They were badly needed. Oxygen Street, for example, was in the Gosta Green area. The local vicar of the Church of St Laurence was the Reverend T. J. Bass. In 1904 he wrote a heart-wrenching account of poverty in his parish called *'Down East Amongst the Poorest'*.

Regarding Oxygen Street he exclaimed 'ye gods, what a name for a street where atmosphere, polluted by neighbouring works made my throat and nose smart and eyes run – the houses were amongst the worst I had ever seen'. A survey of the district of 14 acres showed that only eight were occupied by housing. Here 2,249 people were packed into 589 dwellings, mostly back-to-backs, giving a population density of 272 per acre of inhabited land. This was six times more than the average for the city.

Then in June, 1910, the Council went to approve the purchase of five acres of land from the Lench's Trust that had been cleared for building in Garrison Lane, Bordesley. This was because the existing recreation ground in Coventry Street had been declared insufficient for the needs of the district. The cost was £25,000, with another £2,344 spent on the laying out of the ground. It was completed in October, 1912 and was called Callow Fields Park; locally, however, it was known for some reason as Itchycoo Park.

A yard in Camden Grove, off Camden Drive – very close to where Kathleen Dayus lived. She grew up in conditions such as these. The women on the left are standing outside the communal washhouse, known as a brewus by poor Brummies.

The previous year, the trustees for the charity of the late John Feeney presented to the city the freehold of 1½ acres of land at the corner of Mount Street and Eliot Street in Nechells. Feeney was another wealthy man marked out by his belief in putting something back in to the city in which he had so prospered. He was the son of John Frederick Feeney, the Irish journalist from Sligo who had started the *'Birmingham Daily Post'* with John Jaffray in 1857. It was the younger John Feeney and Jaffray who went on to establish the *'Birmingham Daily Mail'* in 1870.

Nineteen years later they set up the Birmingham Mail Christmas Tree to raise funds for 'toys and cash to brighten the lives of poor children in hospital'. In 1906, the fund began giving out Christmas dinners to poor families and boots to unshod children. Tens of thousands of English Brummies, amongst them my grandparents and great aunts and uncles, owed the shoes on their feet to a charity set up by a second generation Irish Brummie.

John Feeney had other positive and long-lasting effects on Birmingham. When the Art Gallery was opened in 1885 he gave the first instalment of an outstanding collection of works of Japanese enamel, porcelain, lacquer, silver, armour and swords, and also of Chinese bronze, silver and lacquer. This was later supplemented by work from Persia, Turkey, Scandinavia, Germany, France, Spain, Austria and Russia. By 1899 the liberality of John Feeney had led to a collection of 1,693 pieces.

Seven years later when he died, his bequest of the magnificent legacy of £50,000 to the Art Gallery staggered the citizens of Birmingham. This huge sum was crucial for the building of a new Picture Gallery as an extension of the Council House in both Edmund Street and Great Charles Street. These Feeney Galleries were opened in 1912. Feeney's will also left £20,000 to The University of Birmingham, adding to the £5,000 he had given whilst he was alive; £10,000 to the

Unemployed workmen laying out the Mount Street Recreation Ground in 1911.

A superb photo of large numbers of children at the Mount Street Recreation Ground soon after it opened. The large mound at the back was called the Spion Kop after the battle on the hill so named in the South African War.

General Hospital, which swelled the £1,000 handed over previously; and £1,000 each to nine other hospitals and charities.

His obituarist exclaimed with no exaggeration that 'it is hardly possible to exaggerate the importance of this final recognition on Mr Feeney's part of the true duties of citizenship'. Other philanthropic acts whilst he lived included donating £1,000 each to the Women's Hospital, the Coventry and Warwickshire Hospital and the Birmingham Bishopric Fund; and funding the restoration of the Erdington Chapel and its monuments and the carrying out of the entire chancel end of Aston Parish Church.

As for the recreation ground in Nechells, the trustees of Feeney's funds paid for it to be laid out, the land for the building of a pavilion and a keeper's lodge. It was opened on July 24, 1911 by Mrs Feeney. Another and larger recreation ground was also opened in the same year on Mount Street. The site had been transferred from the Public Works Department and was laid out by unemployed workmen, with the Distress Committee paying one-third of their wages. Three years later Brookfields Recreation Ground was opened in George Street.

By now the Parks Department had developed a pioneering scheme that introduced organised games such as skipping, ball games, hopscotch, and ring

Children and officials at the Mount Street Recreation Ground in the 1960s; the Nechells Power Station is in the background.

games on its recreation grounds. It had started in 1910, when the Department had granted facilities to a voluntary committee. The key figure in pushing forward the scheme was Norman Chamberlain, who wanted to ensure that children did not aimlessly wander around recreation grounds.

A cousin of Neville Chamberlain, Norman had become active in social welfare after he returned to Birmingham from Oxford University in 1907. This involvement was informed by his belief in social imperialism, an idea that had taken hold in the aftermath of the South African War of 1899 -1902, during which large numbers of working-class volunteers for the Army had been rejected as physically unfit. Social imperialists were convinced that if the British Empire were to be defended successfully and vigorously then it was vital to improve the character and stamina of Britain's working-class youth. This would be achieved through moral guidance and structured physical activities, so that they would be fit in body and mind.

After setting up a Boys' Club for paper sellers and unemployed boys and young men, in 1911 Chamberlain became involved with the Organised Games held in the recreation grounds of densely-populated and overcrowded areas of Birmingham. In their second year of running, he personally met half the costs of employing experienced teachers as play organisers and instructors. By now, Norman Chamberlain was a councillor and in 1912 he was appointed chairman of the Parks Committee.

Under his leadership it was agreed to allocate £250 of its funds to the Organised Games project. This amount was quickly increased to £564 by 1914, when 22 recreation grounds were included in the scheme. Each had two organisers, one male and one female, who were paid a fee. These people were helped by volunteers who attended on two evenings a week in May, June, and July, and all day during August.

This pioneering work was directed by John Adams of the Birmingham Athletic Institute, who reported with pleasure that the behaviour of the youngsters 'was most creditable. They were good tempered and courteous to each other, respectful to the teachers, honest in the return of material, and truthful in accounting for anything damaged or lost'.

The Parks Committee funded the Organised Games until 1916 when the project was threatened by a lack of funds. It was reinstated after the Bishop of Birmingham expressed his concerns about the importance of promoting good behaviour and healthy physical development in children whose fathers were serving their country in the First World War. Sadly Norman Chamberlain was amongst those who were killed in action.

More happily, the encouragement of organised games continued to be a feature of recreation grounds laid out during the inter-war years – and would carry on doing so until the 1950s. In 1928, the Council took over 7½ acres of a former clay pit close to the St Andrews Ground of Birmingham City. It 'had been under the eyes of the Parks Committee as a desirable site for a much needed open-space in this particular district for some past years'. Unfortunately the financial situation made its purchase and laying out impossible.

Then in 1927 a Birmingham Branch of the National Playing Fields Association was formed largely through the efforts of the Lord Mayor, Alderman A. H. James, and the chairman of the Parks Committee, Councillor G. F. McDonald. Its treasurer was Henry A. Butler and he bought the Kingston Hill spot for £4,000, and then generously presented it to the City with £500 towards the cost of levelling and equipping it. His only condition was that the land should be used as a playground or playing field for all time and for no other purpose.

Kingston Hill Recreation Ground was opened with ceremony on June 27, 1928 by General the Right Honourable the Earl of Cavan. During the course of the official proceedings, the City's Police Band played patriotic and folk music and a programme of organised games was put on by local schoolchildren under the direction of the Education Committee. For boys these included touch rugby, mass bowling, sprints, skittle ball, the high jump, relay races and physical training. As for the girls, they were involved with netball, ling rounders, Danish rounders, hop step

A grown up enjoying a swing at Kingston Hill Recreation Ground in the later 1920s.

and jump, relay races and country dancing. The children's games were followed by a gymnastic display by members of the City's police force.

The 'Souvenir Booklet' of the occasion explained that 'the scheme adopted embodies the most up-to-date features applicable to the development and use of open spaces for public recreation purposes in congested areas'. The Ground contained a children's playground fully equipped with gymnastic apparatus, a sand pit, and a cinder track of four laps to the mile. This track encircled a tar-paved area of 16,000 square yards adapted for organised games for schoolchildren and others; and it was bordered with suitable trees and plants.

A special feature was a pavilion with a dressing room, shelters, store room and lavatories as well as a shelter and conveniences for the children who played on the Ground. In the natural bank facing Kingston Road, an arena had been constructed with terraced seating for 800 people. These facilities had all benefited from the expertise of the Advisory Arts Committee of the Birmingham Civic Society.

During 1928 the Lawson Street Recreation Ground was also opened. There had been a very small open site there since just before the First World War and now it was supplemented by a two-acre Ground that was laid out properly for recreation. Three years later, the Henry Barber Recreation Ground was presented to the City by Dame Martha Constance Hattie Barber through the good offices of the Birmingham Branch of the National Playing Fields Association. She was the widow of Sir Henry Barber, a wealthy solicitor and property developer, and she went on to endow the Barber Institute of Fine Arts at the University of Birmingham. Finally, in March 1932, the Burman Recreation Ground was opened in Bordesley Green by the Lord Mayor, Alderman J. B. Burman. These recreation grounds were dwarfed in size by what would become the City's largest recreation ground: the Lickey Hills.

Chapter 8

Beautiful and Valuable: The Lickey Hills

Lickey Road was the entrance to a world of make-believe for hundreds of thousands of Brummie children. Catching the tram from Navigation Street, they would alight at the terminal and then head off into the Lickey Hills for a day out in the country that was their holiday. Fortified by bottles of cold tea and jam sandwiches wrapped up in pages from the *'Birmingham Mail'*, they would be looked after by Our Wench, their older sister – unless, of course, it was a Sunday and mom and dad had come out with them as well.

They followed in the steps of ancient peoples, for a flint arrow head and a flint scraping tool from the Neolithic period (New Stone Age) have been found on Rednal Hill. After the Norman invasion, the Lickeys were part of the Royal Manor of Bromsgrove and a royal hunting ground. The area was filled with deer and the Normans introduced rabbits that were kept in large enclosures known as warrens, hence Warren Lane. In 1682, Bromsgrove was sold by the crown to the Earl of Plymouth, whose descendants owned much of the Lickeys for the next 250 years.

One of those who was enraptured by the beauty of the unspoilt Lickey Hills was Elihu Burritt, the American consul to Birmingham. In his book, *'Walks in the Black Country'* (1868) he avowed that there were 'no hills more grateful and delightful for airing one's body and soul'. For this peculiar reason they were:

> such happy picnic rendezvous, especially for men, women, and children of the mine and forge district; they are perfectly Scotch in cut and clothing. They are belted with genuine Scotch firs and larches; they are carpeted with genuine Scotch heather, which feels so elastic under your feet and gives such elasticity clear through you to every lock of your hair. The thymy incense of its purple flood of blossom you breathe in the air, and you feel as if on one of the Ochil Hills …
>
> These remarkable hills look as if transplanted here from the Highlands, all in their Highland dress . . . and both for use and ornament they are beautiful and valuable features of the Green Border-Land of the Black Country, and thousands of all ages and conditions from the smoky district luxuriate on these heathered heights in summer. Then they are famous for purple fruits as well as flowers. They supply Birmingham and other large towns far and near with

> bilberries of the finest size and flavour. So, any summer day in the year when the sun shines upon them, these hills are set to the music of merry voices of boys and girls, and older children who feel young on the purple heather at fifty. Then the scenery from these tops embraces a vast sweep of fertile and beautiful country.

In the late nineteenth century the coming of the railway and a station encouraged housing development around Barnt Green and there were concerns that the wondrous Lickeys would be lost to the urban outpouring of Birmingham. These were heightened in 1887 when the new owner of Rednal Hill divided it into building lots to be sold at auction. A local man was stirred to do something to prevent development. He was Mr T. Grosvenor Lee, who Dent praised for at once taking the steps necessary to secure Rednal Hill and 'preserve it in its present wild, forest-like condition for the enjoyment of the public'.

In 1882, as the *'Birmingham Daily Post'* explained, Mr Grosvenor Lee had championed the rights of the public when he had 'sawed a gap in the fence with which the purchaser of the hill had enclosed, it, and so preserved the right of way over it'. Now, and as the secretary of the Birmingham Association for the Preservation of Open Spaces and Public Footpaths, he was instrumental in opening a subscription to raise the money to buy Rednal Hill so that it 'might be made free to the public for ever'.

Richard Cadbury of the chocolate-making business in Bournville was the largest contributor, but with time pressing Mr Grosvenor Lee himself bought about 22 acres of the land for sale. He then went on to agree the purchase of more lots from other buyers, whilst Mr G. Underhill of Small Heath gifted the uncultivated portion of land that he had recently acquired. In May 1888, those plots that had been paid for were handed over to the Baths and Parks Committee.

Just over a year later, Mr Grosvenor Lee announced that the remaining area of Rednal Hill was now ready to be conveyed to the Corporation, to be kept open for ever as a place of public recreation. During this time Lord Windsor, the owner of the Lickey Estate, offered to the Corporation the adjoining Bilberry Hill on a 21-year lease at an annual rental of £5 which he would pay himself. The Council readily accepted.

Dent made the pertinent point that the acquisition of Rednal Hill and Bilberry Hill brought to the Baths and Parks Committee 'property of a character entirely different from any that they had been called upon to deal with previously, in the fact that it was situated at a considerable distance from the town, and depended for its attractiveness upon its being suffered to remain in an uncultivated condition'. Thankfully the Baths and Parks Department rose to the challenge of caring for the hills with skill and care.

Adults and children with donkeys at the tea rooms at the Lickey Hills in the early 1900s.

Its stewardship was extended in 1904 when Barrow Cadbury presented a large piece of land adjoining Bilberry Hill and facing Rednal Hill. He was a worthy descendant of a Quaker family that was marked out by its social concern and action. His father, Richard, and uncle, George, had transformed their business into the largest chocolate and cocoa company in the land. They had done so by adhering to the highest principles and most exacting standards.

The Cadbury name was bound inextricably to quality, purity and fair dealing with their suppliers, customers, workers, and the community in which they prospered. As far back as the 1860s when they were based in the town centre, they had started a Sick Club, introduced half-day working on a Saturday and adopted bank holidays. Often after work they joined the workers in a game of football or cricket, and each morning they held a Bible reading in the stock room.

After they moved their business to 'the factory in a garden' at Bournville in 1879, the Cadbury brothers extended the range of their philanthropic activities. They provided their male and female workers with good wages and recreational facilities; a variety of sporting and other clubs; and educational opportunities, whilst they were also active in the Adult School movement as volunteer teachers.

But the Cadbury liberality was even more wide-ranging. George and his wife, Elizabeth, bought a large house in Northfield and after turning it into an open-air hospital gave it to the Birmingham Cripple's Union. Today it is known as the

Woodlands and is the Royal Orthopaedic Hospital. The couple also paid for schools in Bournville and baths in Stirchley, and they laid the foundations for the internationally-renowned Selly Oak Colleges. They did this with the gift of one of their homes, Woodbroke, as a place for the study of social and religious work in an international atmosphere. In addition George was influential in establishing Fircoft College for Working Men; and of course, he was a leading housing reformer and pioneer of the town planning movement.

Barrow Cadbury was as motivated by concern for the well-being of others. He gave three of his homes to good causes: Uffculme went to the Adult School Union; Cropwood became an Open Air School; and Southfield went to the YMCA. Barrow Cadbury also paid the cost of clearing from the gift of his Lickey site its buildings, which Vince stated had disfigured the landscape. They were replaced with 'a large refreshment hall, with seats for 2,513 visitors, private tea-rooms, bicycle storage, standing for horses and vehicles and other accommodations'. In keeping with his religious beliefs, Barrow Cadbury made one condition – that the Corporation promised that no alcoholic drinks should be sold in the refreshment house.

His generosity was matched by other members of the Cadbury family. In October, 1906, 34 acres at Rednal were given to the Council by Edward Cadbury, George Cadbury the younger, and Henry T. Cadbury, who explained that 'our object

Antonio Tavolier, in the white gown, with his ice-cream cart at the Lickey Hills in the early 1900s. He was born in 1863 in the commune of Atina near to Monte Cassino in southern Italy and he and his wife, Maria Andoni nee Bove, were amongst the pioneers of the Italian community in Birmingham in the late nineteenth century.

in making this offer is to show in some practical form our desire for the welfare of Birmingham, in the government of which our great grandfather, grandfather, and father have successively taken some little part'. This land was connected by a short public path with Rednal and Bilberry Hills, and it included the top of Beacon Hill. This was the highest point of the range and commanded a famous and extensive view.

The Cadburys continued to cherish the Lickeys. In 1913, the freehold of Bilberry Hill was acquired by the City from the Earl of Plymouth (formerly Lord Windsor) for £3,400, and within six years he had sold another 129 acres of wooded heights and pasture. This Rose Hill Estate was acquired by Edward Cadbury and George Cadbury junior and the trustees of the Common Good Trust. They then presented it to the City in 1919. It included the 'Rose and Crown' and ornamental grounds and a lake.

In the following year the Council bought Cofton Hill, Pinefields Woods and the Lickey Warren from the Earl of Plymouth. In total it covered 198 acres and was sold

Sledging on the Lickey Hills in the 1970s.

A mass union meeting at Cofton Park in the 1950s – with workers from the Longbridge car factory.

for £19,000. The Council went on to purchase a further 28 acres, whilst the Cadbury family gifted 29 more. Finally in the late 1920s the Council acquired the 134 acres of Low Hill Farm, opposite the expanding Longbridge car factory, thanks to the will of William Walter Hinde. A Birmingham manufacturer, he had left £10,000 to the Corporation for this purpose and for 'the recreation and pleasure of the people'. It was renamed Cofton Park in 1936.

Chapter 9

Caring for Children: Parks for Balsall Heath, Harborne and Ward End

Louisa Anne Ryland was a woman of noble spirit. One of the greatest philanthropists associated with the City, she was generous with her gifts to Birmingham and to the man who inherited her estates. He was William Charles Henry Alston Smith, the son of Henry Smith, the man she had supposedly loved and been forbidden to marry by her father. Henry had gone on to become Mayor of Birmingham and marry Maria Phipson, a distant cousin of Louisa Anne. In her will she left most her lands to their son on one condition – that he change his name to Charles Smith-Ryland, which he did.

He now owned much of Ladywood and Sparkhill and also the Sparkbrook part of Balsall Heath. The development of the latter area had been so rapid in the 1880s that the farmland and greenery had vanished as if overnight. So sweeping was the march of urbanisation that there was concern that there would be nowhere left for children to play. This part of the Ryland Estate fell under the Balsall Local Board of Health in Worcestershire. The journalist, racing man and character Dyke Wilkinson was a member of the Board and he approached Smith-Ryland to give up some land between the Ladypool Road and Taunton Road as a park.

This idea appealed to the landowner, who said that he would support it elsewhere but not on this property as it 'was ripe for building, too valuable for the purpose'. Then at Derby Day at Epsom, Wilkinson found the winning argument.

> Suppose, Mr Smith-Ryland I had come to you twenty years ago, when you were simply Mr Smith, living a near neighbour to me in Trafalgar Road and I'd said, 'Now, Mr Smith, in twenty years a very rich old lady, not in any way related to you, but for romantic reasons of her own, will leave you her beautiful estate near Warwick, with lots of other real estate, indeed, nearly the whole of her vast wealth, among which is a small farm down Ladypool Road. If all this comes to pass, will you give me a slice of that little farm as a playground for the poor little kiddies of Balsall Heath?' Why you would have said in a moment, 'My dear fellow, if that comes to pass I'll give you the whole bally farm!' Well, Mr Smith-Ryland it has come to pass and I'm begging a little bit of the farm.

Admitting he was bested, Charles Smith-Ryland gave the land for Balsall Heath Park.

In 1891 Balsall Heath was annexed to Birmingham. By that time neither the lease had been signed nor had the boundaries of the park been agreed. Both were soon settled. The original lease was for 21 years at £4 per annum – paid by the landowner himself. He could not then give a longer term as he was tenant for life of the land and his heir was a minor. When Dennis Smith-Ryland did come of age in September 1912, he and his father jointly presented the Park as a free gift to the City, 'thus continuing the liberality of Miss Louisa Anne Ryland'.

A sum of £3,500 was borrowed by the Council for the formation of Balsall Heath Park under a sanction already obtained by the Local Board. Located at the junction of the Ladypool Road and Taunton Road, it was close to the Spark Brook in Stoney Lane and like much of the land hereabouts it was swampy. This meant that the ground had to be raised considerably. Banks planted with shrubs were put up on the sides of the Park where it was overlooked by housing in Birchwood Road and Birchwood Crescent. With 'judicious landscape gardening', the result according to the *'Birmingham Daily Post'* was 'a remarkable amount of picturesqueness for so unpromising a site'.

Children playing at Balsall Heath Park in the late 1960s or early 1970s. It was always known locally as the Little Park and had 'monkey steps', so-called by youngsters, leading up to Birchwood Crescent at the back.

Boasting a large gravelled playground area as well as 'a fair amount of turf and bedding for so small a place', Balsall Heath Park was opened on the May 13, 1893 by the Mayor, Alderman Lawley Parker. He did so by unlocking the main gates with a ceremonial key supplied by the Baths and Parks Committee. Following the official speeches and the playing of music by the Police Band, the Park was thronged all day.

The same year as the opening, members of the Clef Club had begun to organise a series of concerts in Birmingham's parks. Local committees were formed and the Council provided bandstands, but was not allowed by legislation to contribute to the expenses of the events. To overcome this problem a plan adopted in Bradford was followed, whereby the promoters of concerts were permitted to sell programmes and take collections.

Over the next five years, between 200 and 250 concerts were given each summer, with the Police Band performing the most. Crowds flocked in but unfortunately too little money was raised. Accordingly in 1899 the Corporation

The opening of the 'Garden for the Blind' at Queen's Park on July 31, 1953. At the microphone is the blind broadcaster, William Sharp, who performed the opening ceremony. There were also speeches from the Lord Mayor, Alderman G. H. W. Griffith, and the chairman of the Parks Committee, Councillor L. Chaffey.

Crowds of people at Ward End Park soon after its opening in 1904.

acquired the power to spend up to £500 annually on music by way of a clause inserted in the bill authorising the purchase of the private Electric Light Company by the Council.

In the next year, £108 was paid to the Police Band, which had given 120 concerts; thereafter donations were also made to other bands. From 1903, the full allowance of £500 was used to supplement the amount taken by the bands or concert parties from collections, the sale of programmes, and admission fees to the enclosures. After Birmingham was extended in 1911, the allowance was increased to £730 by the Council.

A musical adviser was then engaged and the bands were classified for payments of £2 to £4 for concerts in smaller parks. No payment was made for concerts in the nine large parks, 'in which the audience was trusted to remunerate the performers'. This proved to be unsatisfactory as it meant that regimental bands could not be engaged, whilst many local bands declined to perform in the small parks at the fees offered.

As a result 'a more expensive and elaborate scheme' was adopted. The Police Band was to receive £135 annually, and other local bands between £4 and £6, according to their grade, for each concert. This sum was increased if they gave two concerts on the same day. Special bands were also to be engaged on six Sundays in the summer; whilst concerts were to be given once a week in ten parks, once a fortnight in six, and once a month in nine. These were in addition to those concerts given by the Police Band and the Industrial School Band. All money paid for seats and programmes was to be taken by the Parks Department.

In 1900 the inhabitants of Harborne presented a bandstand to the Council for Queens Park. An octagonal wooden structure, it had a wooden frieze and balustrade with red brick foundations, base, and steps. This bandstand was covered with a slate roof and the whole design was praised in the *'Birmingham Daily Post'* 'as tasteful and pleasing'. It had cost £200, some of which was left over from a fund that had paid for the park and the rest of which had been raised from the Charity Fête Committee.

This had been set up in 1897 after an anonymous donor had given £1,000 to start a public subscription to provide a park in Harborne to commemorate the Diamond Jubilee of Queen Victoria that year. Annexed to Birmingham six years previously from Staffordshire, there was no such facility in the district. The subscription gained wide support and quickly raised £2,300 to buy just less than ten acres of pasture.

On April 29, 1897, Mr H. A. Wiggin, the chairman of the Committee, wrote to the Mayor offering this land to the City. The gift was accepted with on condition that 'children should be particularly cared for, and a portion of the land specially appropriated for their use'. A sum of £2,000 was spent by the Council on laying out the park. It was opened in October, 1898 by the Lord Mayor, Charles Gabriel Beale. Eight years later the park was enlarged by five acres when £2,578 was paid for Court Oak House and its grounds.

In 1953 The Parks Committee paid £1,500 for a 'garden for the blind' on the grass terrace of Court Oak House. This was a gift from the Council to celebrate the recent Coronation of Queen Elizabeth II. It was intended that the Garden would 'supplement the pleasure and enjoyment which sighted persons derive' from the city's parks and Queen's Park was chosen because it was close to the Queen Alexandra College on Court Oak Road, a place that had been set up by the Birmingham Institution for the Blind.

Careful thought went into the design and lay-out of the Garden. Flowers, plants and shrubs were chosen for their scent then labelled in Braille and planted on raised banks so that people could enjoy their smells without stooping. A pergola was covered with jasmines and honeysuckle, whilst the lawn was scented with camomile. There was also a raised pool with a fountain so that visitors could hear the splashing of water; nesting boxes to encourage birds; and a metal embossed plan of the layout to familiarise newcomers.

Harborne had not urbanised as fast as had Balsall Heath and Sparkbrook in the 1880s, but rapid population growth in that decade had been as obvious in Saltley and Washwood Heath. They had also been annexed to Birmingham in 1891 along with the neighbouring districts of Ward End and Little Bromwich. As Vince made plain, East Birmingham had special claims to consideration by the Council for a

Unemployed men paid to excavate and construct the boating pool at Ward End Park in the winter of 1908/09.

new park as 'it was largely occupied by people in the employ of the Corporation', on account of the gas works in Saltley and Nechells.

Consequently, the Baths and Parks Committee were sanctioned 'without any demur' to take two loans. The first for £14,000 was for the purchase of 43 acres of land bordered by the Washwood Heath Road and Sladefield Road; and the second, for £7,850, was used to buy the adjoining Ward End House and its eleven acres of grounds.

Ward End Park was opened on May 14, 1904. It covered 25 acres, with the rest of the acquired land let out for agricultural purposes. In the bad winter of 1908-09, the Distress Committee asked the Council to find work for unemployed workmen. They worked hard and successfully to excavate more than 50,000 cubic yards of earth to build a boating pool. Until the 1960s, a trip to Ward End Park with its pool was a favourite day out for kids from Alum Rock, Ashted, Duddeston, Nechells, Saltley and Washwood Heath.

Three years after the opening of Ward End Park, the Baths and Parks Committee reported that its gardeners were not competent to enforce parks' regulations and deal with disorderly persons. Consequently, in 1907, they were relieved of patrol

Skating on the boating pool at Ward End Park in about 1910.

Boating at Ward End Park in the 1920s; boating ended in the late 1970s.

duty and replaced with a system of police patrol. This was arranged with the co-operation of the Watch Committee for those parks in Birmingham and with county councils for those outside the borough boundaries.

By this date Saltley and hence Adderley Park had become part of the City (as it was from 1889), whilst Calthorpe Park, Highgate Park and Summerfield Park were also within the boundaries. However Aston Park was outside the City and was policed under Warwickshire; whilst Cannon Hill Park was in Kings Norton and was policed under Worcestershire.

Under the scheme the Council paid for fifteen City policemen, three each of the Warwickshire and Worcestershire forces, and one of the Staffordshire force.

In 1907, the annual cost was estimated at £2,000. There was a disadvantage, however, as the policemen 'were not amenable to the authority of the head park-keepers'. In 1912, therefore, a change was made. Under provisions of the Consolidation Act of 1883, the Council appointed park-constables 'who, like the railway police, would be sworn constables having the same legal authority as policemen appointed by

Men and women playing crown green bowls at Ward End Park in the 1960s.

A flower bed at Ward End Park celebrating the Golden Jubilee of the Birmingham Municipal Bank in 1969. Thanks to the late Harold Wareham and his son, Ken.

the Watch Committee'. There were objections that the new force 'would exercise a less efficient control than men trained in police discipline and acting under the direction of the Chief Constable; but the Council approved of the recommendation by a small majority of 43 to 36'. The parks of the annexed districts were soon to be supplemented as a result of an even greater expansion of Birmingham.

Chapter 10

Parks for the Present and Future: Greater Birmingham

It was a red-letter day for Birmingham when the Greater Birmingham Act received the Royal Assent on June 3, 1911. Henceforth its citizens would proudly claim that it was the second city of the Empire, having overtaken Glasgow which had previously held that coveted title. This achievement had come about because of a staggering extension of Birmingham's boundaries. It was to absorb the borough of Aston Manor and the urban district of Erdington from Warwickshire; the urban district of Handsworth from Staffordshire; and the urban districts of Kings Norton and Northfield and the rural district of Yardley, both from Worcestershire.

This annexation would make Birmingham thirteen miles wide at its furthest point and five miles across at its most narrow. Remarkably its area was set to more than treble from just 13,477 acres to 43,568, whilst its population was about to grow significantly by well over half to almost 900,000. In point of fact, with almost a million inhabitants Kolkata was bigger than both Birmingham and Glasgow, but no-one was about to shout that out either in Scotland or the Midlands.

The salient statistics were simple: in size and population Birmingham had eclipsed all its British rivals outside London. Now Birmingham had 50,000 more people than Glasgow and covered over three times as much land. As for Liverpool and Manchester, they had been left trailing in Birmingham's wake. Both had much less than half of its acreage and their populations were noticeably less – by 150,000 and 250,000 respectively.

Such a success had seemed unlikely a decade before when Birmingham had lagged well behind both its northern rivals. No wonder, then, that its triumph was celebrated locally on November 9, 1911 when the act of Parliament authorising the wide extension of the city's boundaries came into force. Flags were flown proudly from public and private buildings across the city, whilst accompanied by numerous city justices, the Lord Mayor, Alderman W. H. Bowater opened the Victoria Law Courts, where all the criminal business of Greater Birmingham would be conducted. Thence the first citizen of the second biggest city in the United Kingdom attended the annual meeting of the City Council, where he was re-elected into his office for the third year in succession.

Six days later, at the first business meeting of the Greater Birmingham City Council, the Lord Mayor announced that George Tangye of the famed hydraulic works had given to the Corporation his unique collection of Boulton, Watt and Murdock relics. It was a most fitting and generous gift on such an auspicious occasion – for it connected the mature city with its heroic age, when it had thrust itself on to the world stage as the city of a 1000 trades and had begun its rapid rise.

Manufacturing had made Birmingham. Renowned for its industrial prowess, it had a thirst for workers. Migrants from the villages of its hinterland in north Warwickshire, north Worcestershire and south Staffordshire were pulled in – as were rural folk from mid Wales, the west of Ireland, the region of Sora in southern Italy, and the Jewish ghettos of the Russian Empire.

Despite differences of ethnicity, belief, and language all were bonded by one thing and one hope: the search for work and a better life. Migration and a high birth rate quickly increased the town's population, a growth accompanied by Birmingham's overflow into neighbouring rural districts to grab space for building.

Quickly they fell to urbanisation. In 1832 Birmingham became a parliamentary borough. It also included Edgbaston from Warwickshire and Deritend, Duddeston and Nechells, which had been part of Aston in the same county. Six years later all were included in the new municipal borough of Birmingham. Then in 1891, Balsall Heath was brought in from Worcestershire; Harborne from Staffordshire; and Saltley, Little Bromwich and Ward End from Warwickshire. They were followed by Quinton, which was taken from Halesowen in 1909.

All were important extensions that accelerated Birmingham's emergence as a major city. Yet none had been as audacious as the extension of 1911. Such a bold move was envied by Manchester, which had long sought to have Salford pulled in to its orbit. It was made possible by a council that revelled in the title of 'the best governed city in the world', bestowed upon it by the American journalist, Julian Ralph in 1890.

His praise stemmed from the highly successful mayoralty from 1873-76 of the brilliant Joseph Chamberlain – but even after he switched to national politics in the latter years, a spirit of ambition continued to possess the Council, particularly with regard to Birmingham's status. In 1884, the first Birmingham Assizes were held; in 1887 Queen Victoria laid the foundations of the Law Courts in the newly developed Corporation Street; on January 14, 1889 a Royal Charter raised Birmingham to a city; and then in 1896, Councillor James Smith became the first Lord Mayor of Birmingham.

These expressions of dignity were reflected in ambitious council policies that impacted positively on Birmingham's national and international image. They included the municipalisation of the local electric supply in 1899 and of the tramways in 1903; and the opening of the municipality's Elan water supply a year later. Such notable achievements were matched by other developments that emphasised the waxing confidence of Birmingham. In 1900 a Royal Charter was granted to found the University of Birmingham, making it the first civic university in England. Nine years later its new buildings in Edgbaston were opened by King Edward VII and Queen Alexandra – by which date Birmingham had been an Anglican diocese since 1905.

Parks were a significant aspect of Birmingham's municipal activities and enhanced its civic pride. Their number continued to expand following the City's extension and led to the separation of the Baths and Parks Committee into two separate committees each with its own department. By this date Birmingham already owned Aston Park, and the local authority of Aston had not added any parks itself; whilst Handsworth, formerly in Staffordshire, brought with it just one – Victoria Park.

Its founding has been researched in detail by Simon Baddeley, who makes it clear that the park was not a charitable bequest. It arose because 'community leaders persuaded the taxpayers of Handsworth to finance the largest loan ever raised in the district'. To do so, they had to overcome stiff opposition.

The battle for the park had begun in January 1882 at a meeting of the Handsworth Local Board when one of its members, Austin B. Lines, raised 'the subject of a recreation ground for the district'. He pointed out that the area had 25,000 people, 26 miles of streets, and 3,700 acres – not one of which was dedicated to the inhabitants for recreation. Lines proposed, therefore, that a public park or pleasure ground should be provided. A committee of four members of the board was appointed to take the proposal forward.

As Simon Baddeley's research reveals, the Grove Lane Estate was offered to the Board for £10,000, but this price was deemed too high and the issue of cost was to become a contentious one. Over the next few years, the matter of a park was raise again by Austen Lines, but it was not until 1887 that a public campaign arose. On January 1, 1887 an editorial in the *'Handsworth News'* was headed 'A Handsworth "Lung"'.

The editor looked forward to the purchase of a public park in an area that was increasing rapidly in population and where land was growing dearer and more difficult to obtain because of urbanisation. The children of the poor needed 'a recreation ground away from the dangers and temptations of the streets'; whilst their elders required 'a promenade tastefully arranged and carefully kept, to which, after the fatigues of the day, they can resort for change and rest'. And to everyone in Handsworth, a park would mean 'the preservation of a large and important plot of land from the ravages of the speculative builder and the enrichment of the district by the acquisition of something of real beauty and utility'.

Part of the Grove Estate was hoped to become the park. A few days after the editorial, Mr T. H. Pearson proposed that the Board buy 20 acres of the estate for £7,500 for a public park, subject to the approval of the ratepayers. He was supported by Austen Lines and by Joseph Wainwright, who stated that now that the sanitary work of the Board was nearing completion it would be feasible to borrow the amount needed and also to make an appeal to wealthy inhabitants for the £2,500 to lay out the park.

The motion was carried by ten votes to one, but opponents of spending money on a public park began a virulent letter-writing campaign to the local press. The chief objection, as in Birmingham in the 1850s, was based on cost and the resultant increase in the rates. At a rowdy ratepayers' meeting on January 18, 1887, one opponent declared that those in favour of the park were actually the voice of Birmingham and not the voice of Handsworth. This opened up a political division. Local Conservatives believed that Handsworth's Liberals, who dominated the Board, were having their strings pulled by Chamberlain's supporters.

Despite vehement objections, the resolution for the purchase of the land for the park was passed 'much to the disgust of many' in the room. The Board went on to agree to buy the land and apply to the local government board to borrow £7,600 to do so. This provoked an 'anti-parkite' to write to the 'Birmingham Daily Gazette', a Conservative newspaper. He urged Handsworth's Conservative Association to organise against the Liberals on the Local Board with 'their excessive taxation, neglected thoroughfares, impure gas, and radical nostrums' and their plan to impose the 'perpetual burden of a park for the exclusive advantage of no other than the non-taxpaying classes'. This argument ignored the fact that property owners included the rates in the rents that they charged working-class tenants for their houses.

The Board members carried on regardless and Joseph Wainwright set up a Public Park Fund in honour of Queen Victoria's Golden Jubilee. He pronounced 'what better thing could we do than to provide a beautiful park for the present and future use of the inhabitants of the district, thousands of whom would not except for such provision have any fit place at hand in which to enjoy an hour's outdoor recreation'.

Yet the 'anti-parkites' were not done. They sent a petition with 2,000 names to the Local Government Board opposing any loan to Handsworth to pay for a public park. The national body decided that a government inspector would hold an inquiry before any monies could be sanctioned. It took place on March 17, 1887 at the Public Buildings on the Soho Road. The Board's clerk emphasised that the loan would not lead to an increase in the rates and noted that the workmen at Tangye's hydraulic works just across the border in Smethwick had passed a resolution in favour of the park's scheme.

The opposition was led by a Conservative, Mr W. M. Ellis. He made it plain that many local residents were clerks who were employed in Birmingham and that presently 'they have great difficulties to make both ends meet and if the rates could be reduced it would be a great boon to them'. This was an acute observation. Just three years before, in 1884, the franchise had been extended, and since then the Conservatives nationally led by Disraeli had begun to gain widespread support amongst the lower middle-class. Most clerks came from the more prosperous ranks of the working-class and feared dropping into poverty and losing their precarious status. Their worries over a rate rise were very real to them.

Soon after the public enquiry was held, so too were the elections for four members of the Handsworth Board. One of the seats was that of a retiring member. In a conciliatory move the Liberals decided to put forward only its three candidates who were standing for re-election. This allowed them to offer the vacated seat to the Conservatives. If there were no other candidates this would mean eight Liberals and four Conservatives on the Board – a course of action that had been advocated by the *'Handsworth News'*. On March 5, its editorial explained that 'as there seems every probability of sufficient money being contributed voluntarily to lay out the park the Conservative party might consent to withdraw their opposition to the purchase of the land'.

The Conservatives seem to have accepted this approach and nominated A. A. Ellis. This move did not appease the 'anti-parkites' who put forward George Blackham as an anti-park candidate. Surprisingly he was a Liberal but came forward as an independent nominated by a leading member of the Conservative Party locally. He came bottom of the poll in early April, and according to the *'Handsworth News'* suffered a 'crushing defeat'. Days later the Local Government Board wrote to the Conservative, Mr W. M. Ellis stating they had no sufficient reason to refuse to comply with the application for a loan made by the Handsworth local board and so sanctioned it. (For this discussion, I pay tribute to the work of Simon Baddeley in *'The Founding of Handsworth Park, 1882-1898'*, 1997).

The Grove Estate was then bought and laid out as Victoria Park, so named in honour of the Queen. It was opened on Wednesday June 21, 1888 but according to the *'Birmingham Daily Post'*, the celebrations were marred by a continuous downfall of rain. Still this did not stop the gathering of a large crowd. The event began at 3.30 pm when a procession left the Board's offices. It included a detachment of the Handsworth Volunteers and their band, a number of Staffordshire Constabulary and members of the Board.

At the park's entrance in Grove Lane, silver keys to its gates were presented to the present and former chairmen of the board – Austen Lines and Joseph Wainwright. Of course, both had been staunch supports of the park. After a hymn had been sung and a prayer of dedication offered, Lines declared the park open 'as a place of recreation for the people forever'. He observed that as he had predicted, since the purchase land values hereabouts had risen considerably as new roads were laid out; but in a generous gesture to those who had opposed the park he hoped that they could now see its use and he gave them credit for the best motives.

A decade later, on March 30, 1898, the Victoria Park Extension was opened. This consisted of 35 acres of land. Then in 1911, when Handsworth became part of Birmingham its park was renamed Handsworth Park. Vince explained that this was 'in deference to the superior claims to the royal title possessed by the park at Small Heath, which had been visited by the Queen in 1887, and named after her by her own royal command'.

Handsworth Park soon became well-known for its flower shows. As early as September 1836, a Grand Dahlia Flower Show had been held in Birmingham and within 20 years flower societies had sprung up across the town and its surrounding district. They included the Handsworth and Lozells Floricultural Society which was soon attracting several thousand people to its yearly flower shows in various locations.

The first annual flower show held at Handsworth Park was in 1900 and it was opened by the famous novelist, Marie Corelli. This was a coup for Handsworth as she sold more books than other popular contemporaries such as Arthur Conan Doyle, H. G. Wells, and Rudyard Kipling. One reporter waxed lyrical about these Handsworth Park flower shows, hailing them as 'the mecca of every horticulturalist', whilst 'the flowers and surroundings are a natural attraction which pleases the eye, bewildered with the more flamboyant beauties of the flower tent.

Tennis lessons at Handsworth Park in the 1930s.

The Sons of Rest at Handsworth Park in the 1950s. This organisation had been started in Birmingham in 1927 to promote leisure and social activities for men over 60. By 1950 the idea had spread to other places like Worcester and in Birmingham it had 33 branches with 2,000 members. Those at Handsworth met in this specially-designed brick building that replaced an old timber structure.

No language could properly visualise to the reader the riot of colour, the wealth of bloom, the kaleidoscope of tints and the sensuous beauty of the exhibits'.

After Handsworth became part of Birmingham in 1911, the organising Society changed its name to the Birmingham Horticultural Society. This was the same year that the first Chelsea Show was held by the Royal Horticultural Society. The Handsworth Park flower shows continued each year until the Second World War, when they were discontinued.

They were revived in 1947 by the Parks Committee, which decided to organise a two-day Birmingham Flower show. It also included a single breed dog show, a section for bees and honey, a rabbit show, fun fair, military bands and talent shows. A year later horse jumping was added and the name of the event was changed to the City of Birmingham Show.

By 1950 there were eight classes in the flower show itself: open; amateur; allotment; gentlemen gardeners; begonia; ladies; children; and municipal. There was also a caged bird show and the two-day event was rounded off on the last evening with

The horse show at the City of Birmingham Show in Handsworth Park in the 1950s.

The dog show at the City of Birmingham Show in Handsworth Park in the 1950s.

Scottish dancers at the City of Birmingham Show in the 1960s.

Tossing the caber at the City of Birmingham Show in the 1970s.

Princess Margaret takes the salute at the Birmingham Scout Rally in Handsworth Park in 1966.

community singing, a fireworks display by Wilder's of Greet, and the singing of the National Anthem. So successful did the Birmingham Show become that by 1969 'the park was bursting at the seam with over 18,000 entries'. Accordingly the next year it was moved by the Parks Committee to the 100-acre Perry Park.

The strong views that had been aroused in Handsworth for and against the provision of a public park were absent in the Rural District of Yardley. Here Birmingham Council inherited several recreation grounds. These were in Acocks Green, Greet, Stechford, Yardley, Morden Road in Stechford, and Red Hill in Hay Mills. They ranged in size from three to eight acres. In addition Yardley boasted a nineteen-acre park at Sparkhill. Opened in 1904 it had been donated by Yardley Great Charity, a large landowner in the district.

During the 1950s many Irish families settled in Sparkhill and the Park became important to them, as Steve McCabe made plain:

> We lived in Castleford Road and all my early memories revolve around that house and the surrounding area. The back garden was, of course, sufficient most of the time. However, the place that every kid wanted to be was Sparkhill Park. It was

where I learned to ride my bike. It was a place to meet others. I can remember being there in summer and seeing lots of other families who would meet there to talk about the recent events and what was happening 'at home' in Ireland.

For children, Sparkhill Park was a place where you could feel free (surrounding roads were a lot less busy then). There was the playing equipment, which is still located at the top end behind the baths; that required money and was a 'special treat'. The bandstand could be imagined as a spaceship or base, which some would attack and others defend. I don't remember a band playing there. It's probably a good thing because we kids wouldn't have welcomed intruders with musical instruments!

Those younger than forty probably won't remember that there used to be a paddling pool that occupied much of the bottom end of the park closest to Springfield. In summer you'd get in and splash about with whoever else happened to be there. (Carl Chinn, *'Birmingham Irish, Making Our Mark'*, 2003)

To the north of Sparkhill, the inclusion of Erdington within Birmingham brought with it a small piece of land at the Oval and larger spaces at Short Heath Park,

Adults and children in Sparkhill Park in the 1950s.

A super photo taken by the late Harold Wareham in May 1968 and showing the flower beds in front of Rookery House at Rookery Park in Erdington. Thanks to his son, Ken.

Brookvale Park and Rookery Park. This latter had been the grounds of Rookery House. Originally called Wood End Green House, it had been built in about 1727 by Abraham Spooner. He was an ironmonger, someone who bought the goods made by manufacturers and sold them on the world stage. Based in Edgbaston Street in the heart of the town he also purchased property, loaned money to smaller-scale businessmen himself, and arranged for loans through other wealthy citizens.

Interestingly Abraham's granddaughter, Barbara Spooner, married the anti-slavery campaigner, William Wilberforce and the two lived in the house for a time. After passing to another family, in 1903 Rookery House was bought by Erdington Urban District and was used as its Council House. Subsequently its grounds, including a beautiful Italian Garden, were opened as Erdington's first public park.

Six years later Brookvale Park was opened. This had been Lower Witton Lake and it had an important history. Fresh water is often regarded as a basic human right and sadly just as often it is out of the reach of the poor. So it was in Birmingham until Joseph Chamberlain took control of Birmingham in 1873. Under his revolutionary new regime, the private water companies were municipalised and landlords were forced to close polluted wells and connect their properties via a standpipe to the town water supply.

Sailing miniature boats at Brookvale Park in the 1950s.

Dr Hill, the Medical Officer of Health, was enjoined to inspect the wells of Birmingham. The results were damning. In almost all instances, the hundreds of wells inspected were polluted with sewage, through surface drainage, which rendered the water unfit for drinking. As a result, in the nine years from 1876 almost 3,000 wells supplying about 60,000 people were closed.

As for the town water, it was taken from the supplies of the private Birmingham Waterworks Company. This was authorised by an Act of Parliament in 1826 to cover Birmingham and the Parish of Aston. The company developed slowly, taking five years to make a reservoir at Aston for water from the River Tame. By 1859, water was also taken from the Hawthorn Brook in Witton and the Perry Brook.

Over the next decade or so the company extended its operations but despite its growth, the Birmingham Waterworks Company was faced by major problems. In particular its water was collected from various sources over a wide area and was stored in twelve reservoirs: three in Witton; two each in Aston, Edgbaston and at Plant's Brook; and one each in Perry and Whitacre. These reservoirs led to an expensive pumping system. For all its engineering achievements and its desire to increase Birmingham's supply of fresh water, by 1875 when it was municipalised, the private water company had only 17,641 customers. This situation changed drastically following the takeover of the water supply by the City.

Chamberlain justified the action by stressing that the health of large towns and the liability of their populations were connected intimately with the water supply, whilst there were special reasons why the supply of water 'to all communities should be in the hands of local representative authorities, and not in the hands of private speculators, to whom pecuniary profit must necessarily be the first consideration'. Moreover he asserted that 'the waterworks should never be a source of profit, as all profit should go in reduction at the price of water'.

Over the next few years, improvements were made to the town's supply, including a new reservoir at Shustoke, but increasingly the Council became aware of the difficulties with the local supply. Consequently in 1890 the Council was forced to look elsewhere for its supplies. It settled upon the water from the Elan and Claerwen rivers in Wales, to be gathered in reservoirs created by great dams. The first at Claerwen was opened by King Edward VII in July 1904. This event ensured that the Lower Witton Lake was no longer needed as a reservoir and allowed it to be bought by Erdington Urban District and turned into a park.

To the south-west of Birmingham, the urban district of Kings Norton and Northfield also possessed parks that were brought into Birmingham in 1911. The first of them was Selly Oak Park. It was the gift of Emma Joel Gibbins and her four sons, William, Thomas, John and Benjamin. Emma was the youngest daughter of Richard Tipper and Elizabeth Cadbury and she and her sons were the owners of the Birmingham Battery Metal Company. A significant concern, it had begun in Digbeth but by 1895 was focused on a refinery and rolling mill at Selly Oak.

Determined to provide an open space for their workers, they gave over eleven acres of the Weoley Park Estate as a park. It was opened on Easter Monday, April 3, 1899. Thousands gathered to watch as the 88 year old Emma Gibbins open the gates with a silver key and then listen to speeches by the donors and local dignitaries.

In his deeply researched book on the park, Ken Pugh reveals that in its first year it was used for the Oddfellows and Foresters Amalgamated Juvenile Fête; the annual Selly Oak and Bournbrook Children's Fête; the annual Selly Oak Horticultural Show; an unspecified event for the Order of Rechabites, a temperance organisation; and sports, staged by the Selly Oak Victoria Brass Band. Selly Oak Park was later enlarged by two more gifts of land from the Gibbins family in 1913 and 1922 so that it stretched across Gibbins Road to the canal. (Ken Pugh, *'The Heydays of Selly Oak Park'*, 2010).

Nearby is Muntz Park, lying between Umberslade Road and Gristhorpe Road. It is named after Frederick Ernest Muntz who gave three acres of farmland to the district council in May 1905 to be used as a park. Over the next four years, the council brought two more acres from him. Interestingly, he was the grandson of George Muntz, the industrialist who was one of the first two MPs for Birmingham after the Great Reform Act of 1832.

Crowds looking down at musicians playing in The Dell at Muntz Park in the late 1920s. In 1923 the Birmingham Civic Society had granted £300 to re-landscape the park. As part of this programme an amphitheatre was created, it was called The Dell and had a paved central area for dancing and a raised platform for performers.

Of course, Muntz had also spoken at the public meeting held at the Town Hall on November 19, 1844 'to consider the propriety of establishing Public Baths and the formation of Public Walks and other places of recreation for the inhabitants'. He had also spoken on July 26, 1853, at the meeting 'to take into consideration a project providing a public park for the inhabitants' of Birmingham. Muntz's son, George Frederick, went on to donate £1,000 to the fund that led to the purchase of Aston Hall and Park by Birmingham, and it seems fitting that his grandson gave land for a park in Selly Oak.

Another important acquisition by the urban district of Kings Norton and Northfield lay to the east in Kings Heath. I have lived in and around this area all my life and from when I was a child I was aware that my family had a longstanding connection with it, and that I walked where my ancestors had walked. But I had no idea quite how longstanding and how deep was that connection until recently.

From family stories I knew that my great grandfather, Richard, had gone to Moseley National School, as did myself and my brother, Darryl. In our childhood in the 1960s it was surrounded by houses but in his day in the 1870s it had lain in the midst of the Worcestershire countryside. I also knew that Richard's father, Henry, had farmed somewhere in King's Heath and that he had died in a farming accident – but I did not realise that whenever I step along the High Street or go around Kings Heath Park, or shop in Sainsbury's that I am stepping alongside my ancestors.

Why? Because my great, great, great grandfather, Henry Chinn and his wife, Ann, nee Barwell rented the 88 acre Church Farm in Kings Heath for many years. The 1840 Tithe Map indicates that his farm house was on the Alcester Road, where Sainsbury's now stands. Henry was a tenant of William Congreve Russell, one of the biggest landowners in Moseley and Kings Heath. It was he who had the grand Georgian Kings Heath House in Kings Heath Park built in 1832.

Henry Chinn was able to pass his tenancy of Russell's land on to his son, also Henry. Unhappily the fortunes of the family changed badly for the worse in 1868 when the younger man was made bankrupt. It must have been a bitter pill for Henry the elder to swallow. As he came to the end of his life his life's work in raising his family's position to one of comfort and security had been shattered. He died in 1873 at the old age of 80 and was buried at St Mary's, Moseley – as had been his mother, father and wife. Worse was to come for his family.

His bankrupt son, Henry the younger, had quickly found work as a farm bailiff with the Cartlands of The Priory. This house now belongs to King Edward's Camp Hill School and lies just behind Kings Heath Park. Henry lived with his wife and children just by the Park in a cottage on Vicarage Road. It was not the life of a

A boy sitting in Kings Heath Park about 1914.

Children playing on the swings at Victoria Common in Northfield in the 1950s. This was laid out on common land formerly called Bradley's Field by the Kings Norton and Northfield Urban District after George Cadbury had gifted the four-acre site in 1897. It was so-named as it was intended to have it opened to mark the Diamond Jubilee of Queen Victoria that year; however the project was not completed until 1901. The area was extended by two acres in 1913 thanks to George Cadbury, and by another six acres between 1928-32 through the gifts of Mrs E. M. Cadbury, Edward Cadbury and the Bournville Village Trust.

prosperous tenant farmer but it was still a good job that was far better than that of an agricultural labourer. Then tragedy struck in 1877. The family story goes that Henry fell off a haystack and broke his neck. He was 54 and was buried at All Saints Church, Kings Heath.

Whatever the cause of death, it was a disaster for his widow, Mary Anne. She had five children aged twelve and under, but with no man she lost both his income and her home – for the cottage had gone with the job. Mary Anne must have been a strong and determined woman for she kept her family together and out of the hated workhouse. Putting what belongings she had on a hand cart she traipsed to nearby

Sparkbrook, then part of Balsall Heath, and rented a back house in White Street, close to where Balsall Heath Park would be laid out.

Here Mary Anne scratched a living as a washerwoman. Her ability to cope against adversity meant that she got by; though she and her children, including my great grandfather, Richard, knew what it was to be clammed and to have to scrat to survive. Having worked to keep her family out of the hated workhouse, she died in 1910, still living in White Street and still a widow.

Two years before, Kings Norton and Northfield Urban District had paid £11,000 for what would become half of the present Kings Heath Park. The vendor was a trust set up by the Cartlands, who had bought the house that had been built for Congreve Russell and the land around it. This trust sold the remaining half of the grounds to Birmingham Corporation for £5000 in 1914, and this area was immediately incorporated into Kings Heath Park.

During the inter-war years, Kings Heath had many facilities including football and cricket pitches, three grass tennis courts, two crown green bowling greens, one putting green, glasshouses, a pool, ornamental gardens, a tea room and public toilets. Like other parks in Birmingham, it was highly popular, especially for families at weekends and bank holidays.

After the Second World War there was a move towards self-sufficiency and to train gardeners because of a major skills shortage. This led to the Council developing the School of Horticultural Training at Kings Heath House from 1953. Since 1995 an exciting partnership with Pershore and Bournville Colleges has enabled the training centre at Kings Heath Park to develop a more diverse range of courses both professionally and for the amateur.

Students use as a training ground the Television Gardens. These were started at Kings Heath Park 1972 in partnership between Birmingham City Council and ATV (later Central Television). The programme 'Gardening Today' was originally devised to show viewers how to design and maintain their gardens and the first presenters were Bob Price and Cyril Fletcher. The garden of one-third of an acre was later extended and many programmes were made there.

Chapter 11

Playing Fields and Parks: The Inter-War Years

Just below Aston Park stands the cathedral-like and magnificent Aston Parish Church. Mostly a Victorian structure, its tower dates from the late fifteenth century and it includes intriguing relics that have survived from even earlier. The oldest effigy is of a knight resting. Carved in alabaster in the armour of the fourteenth century, it is believed to represent Sir Ralph Arden who died about 1360. His feet lie upon a boar and beside him is the sandstone effigy of a lady.

Some accounts state that she is Sir Ralph's wife, Isabel de Bromwich, but it is more likely that she is Elizabeth de Clodeshale, brought to mind in Clodeshall Road, Alum Rock. During the Wars of the Roses her husband, Robert Arden, was captured whilst recruiting men against the king and was killed – thus becoming one of the first men to be die in that conflict. Aston Parish Church also has a stained glass window depicting Walter Arden (who died in 1502) and his wife, Dame Alianore. In the tracery, the ornamental stone open-work above the window, there is a bear and ragged staff. This was the long-standing badge of the Ardens and consequently became the symbol of Warwickshire.

Above and below Walter and Alianore are the coats of arms of families that were either connected with or married into the Ardens. They begin with that of Arden of Wilmcote (near Stratford) and end with that of Shakespeare. This is because Walter Arden is believed by many to have been the great-grandfather of Mary Arden, Shakespeare's mother.

The Ardens are one of the most curious families in England. They traced their descent from Ulwin, whose father was the Danish holder of Warwick and whose mother was the sister of Earl Leofric of Mercia. As Ulwin did not join King Harold at the Battle of Hastings he was allowed to keep his lands by the Norman victor, William the Conqueror, and his son is recorded in the Domesday Book of 1086 as Turchill de Warwick.

He soon lost Warwick but retained many manors, and two years later another document gives him as Turchill Eardene. Apparently his surname derives from the Forest of Arden, which covered much of north Warwickshire and in which lay most of his properties. Amongst them were the Pipe Lands, now Pype Hayes Park. The

The formal gardens at Pype Hayes Park in the 1960s.

Ardens themselves lived at Park Hall, Castle Bromwich and their direct male line died out in 1643 with a Robert Arden. His lands were divided amongst his sisters. The youngest, Anne, was married to Sir Charles Adderley and they gained Saltley. It was their descendant who gifted Adderley Park. The third of them, Dorothy, was married to Hervey Bagot and she took with her Pype Hayes.

Like the Ardens, the Bagots are a fascinating family. Established in Staffordshire from the eleventh century, since 1360 their main residence has been Blithfield Hall – but as a younger son Hervey Bagot needed somewhere to live with his wife, Dorothy. Consequently his father had Pype Hayes Hall built for them. This impressive Jacobean mansion and its grounds remained in the possession of the junior branch of the Bagots until the early twentieth century. Then in 1920 the trustees of the Bagot family sold both the hall and 76 acres of the estate for £10,000 to Birmingham Corporation. This became Pype Hayes Park, which was enlarged in 1928 by the purchase of the remainder of the estate for £3,016.

Covering 113 acres, this was the second-largest park acquired by Birmingham during the inter-war years after Cofton Park. Third in size came the 86 acres of

Senneleys Park in Bartley Green. Formerly farm land it was bought in 1935 and opened a year later. Slightly smaller was Highbury Park with 75 acres. Fittingly given his belief in the importance of the municipality and the facilities it provided for its citizens, this had been the estate of Joseph Chamberlain, who lived in a grand house called Highbury. Some of the estate was leased from Richard Cadbury, who lived nearby at Uffculme, but after Chamberlain died in 1914 his family left Highbury.

Seven years later the Highbury Trustees rented fifteen acres of the estate to the Council for a nominal rent of £1 a year; and later that year the General Purposes Committee transferred to the Parks Committee fifteen acres of the Uffculme estate on condition that both portions would be laid out as a park. Then in October 1922, the Birmingham Civic Society bought the adjoining 42-acre estate called the Henburys for £9,000 and generously presented it to the City.

An active and important organisation, two years previously the Society had also given to Birmingham the ten-acre Daffodil Park in Northfield. At Highbury, a further gift of three acres soon followed and by 1933 the Park covered 77 acres – a portion of which was laid out as athletic fields. Once again the Civic Society made a valuable contribution, helped by a donation of £1,000 by Barrow Cadbury.

Cross country cycling at Highbury Park in the 1970s.

Although dominated by grassland, Highbury Park embraces an enchanting array of features such as ancient hedgerows, marshland, ornamental trees, woodland plants, streams, pools, shrubs, woodland and scrub. In 1975, it was one of the parks and open spaces investigated by W. G. 'Bunny' Teagle in his report for the Nature Conservancy Council. This was called *'The Endless Village'* because in 1843 the Midland Mining Commission had described the Black Country as 'an interminable village'.

Focusing on Birmingham and the Black Country, Teagle's work had a significant and positive impact. It was one of the first studies of an industrial conurbation and it influenced nature conservancy work across the urban United Kingdom. Regionally it resulted in the formation of the Urban Wildlife Group. Highbury Park continues to be a notable open space and part of it has been recognised as a 'Site of Local Importance for Nature Conservation' by the government body, English Nature, and Birmingham City Council.

At 45 acres in extent, Salford Park, Aston was the fifth largest park acquired by Birmingham during the period between the World Wars. It came in two parts: one in 1919 and the other four years later. Much of it was the former reservoir of the City's Waterworks Department and the rest had been filter beds that had been converted into open spaces alongside the Lichfield Road. These were to provide facilities for tennis, athletics and other games.

Crowds on the banks of the reservoir at Salford Park watching canoeists in the 1970s.

Looking for tiddlers and jack bannocks at a stream in Swanshurst Park in the 1960s.

Across the city on its south side, Moseley New Pool was bought by the Council for £31,500 in 1917. Six years later more additions were made to this space, including twelve acres presented by the Birmingham Common Good Trust – one of the several good causes set up by the Cadburys. With this gift the name of the sixteen-acre area was changed to Swanshurst Park. The seven acres of Bournville Park in Linden Road that came to the City in 1920 also arose from a Cadbury charity, in this case the Bournville Village Trust. In 1946 the Trust would also gift the twelve acres of the Valley Parkway in Bournville Lane. This included an attractive model yachting pool and was already laid out – as was the almost eight acres of Woodlands Park that was donated to the City two years later.

The other most prominent Quaker family in Birmingham were the Lloyds of banking fame. Of course, Thomas Lloyd had been a vital figure in the saving of Aston Park and Hall and in 1919 Alderman John Henry Lloyd and his wife gifted the Farm and its grounds of just over nine acres to the City. This had been the home of the Lloyds since the 1740s. Once part of a 56 acre estate, it was now the centre of a middle-class enclave surrounded by working-class streets. A former Lord Mayor of Birmingham, Alderman Lloyd hoped that the grounds would be used as an open space for recreation and that the old name would be retained. Both suggestions were readily accepted.

Happy days at Farm Park in the 1960s.

Within a few years of this gift, private developers and the Council had built scores of thousands of new homes upon the farmland that had been brought into the City by the extension of 1911. Fortunately the local authority recognised the need for open spaces in these extensive new districts and in particular reacted positively to the campaigning of the National Playing Fields Association.

This was formed in 1925 by Brigadier-General Reginald Kentish so as to provide healthy recreational opportunities for local communities throughout the United Kingdom. It had impressive support, with the Duke of York, later King George V, as its first President. The Birmingham Branch, the Birmingham Playing Fields Association, was especially active in initiating schemes for the acquisition of land for recreation. It was responsible for the Kingston Hill Recreation Ground – and it also paid for some playing fields.

In 1928, through its treasurer, Henry A. Butler, it gave seventeen and half acres for the Wake Green Playing Fields in Moseley. The next year the Birmingham Playing Fields Association itself gifted 24½ acres in Wagon Lane for the Lyndon Playing Fields – later extended by seven acres transferred from the Public Works

Department. The association was as effective in working with other organisations such as the Birmingham Common Good Trust, the Trident Trust, the Bournville Village Trust and the Birmingham Civic Society so as to provide grants to buy and lay out other parks, recreation grounds and open spaces.

And as in the past, publicly-spirited citizens continued to play a significant role with gifts of land or money. The first to do so was Alderman Sir George Kenrick. In 1918, seven years before the national body for playing fields emerged, he gave land at Pebble Mill in Edgbaston. Five acres were for the general public; whilst ten acres were for the exclusive use of children attending elementary schools under the jurisdiction of the City's Education Department – of which Kenrick himself was then chairman.

Originally from Wales, the Kenricks had settled in Birmingham in the later 1700s and had become wealthy through manufacturing hollowware in West Bromwich. Unitarians, they had worshipped at the Church of the Messiah alongside Joseph Chamberlain. Indeed his first wife was Harriet Kenrick and after her death he married her cousin, Florence, who similarly died tragically. As for Sir George Kenrick, his munificence also included £25,000 towards the building of

Children in Grove Park, Harborne in the 1970s.

The Annual Inspection of Kings Norton Park on July 25, 1952. Thanks to Del Wilford.

In 1937, Douglas D. James presented to the City 57 acres of land at Sheldon. He dedicated the site as part of the national memorial to the memory of King George V, who had died the previous year. It was agreed that fifteen acres should be laid out as school playing fields and the remainder as a recreation ground. This photo shows the site before work began – and in the background is the parish church of St Giles. The project was not completed until after the Second World War.

Birmingham University at Edgbaston and £18,000 for a Chair in physics, and £26,000 for the West Bromwich School of Art.

In 1933 his cousins, G. W. Kenrick and Alderman Byng Kenrick, made another gift to the City. Their father, the Right Honourable William Kenrick, had lived at 'The Grove' in Harborne for 40 years and had stated that when his descendants ceased to live there he wanted the house and its 24 acres passed to the City. This was now done, subject to an existing lease to Alderman Kenrick for his lifetime and to his wife should she survive him. The only other condition was that the land should be used substantially and maintained as an open space with, hopefully, the name of 'The Grove'. This was agreed to.

Two years after the handover of the Pebble Mill Playing Fields, in 1920, the Trident Trust gave 25 acres on the Redditch Road at Kings Norton for playing fields

A day out at Trittiford Park in the 1930s. The fifteen acres of Titterford Mill Pool and land were transferred by the Housing Committee to the Parks Committee with a value of £1,200 in 1923. The name had been Titterford, but it was changed to Trittiford by the council supposedly because the original form was deemed vulgar.

Playing rugby at Daisy Farm in Highters Heath in the 1950s. Its 24 acres were transferred by the Estates Committee in 1931 for £3,250.

Father Murphy's (All Wexford) Hurling Team, 1961 at Glebe Farm. Opened as playing fields in 1932, this was the favoured venue for the Gaelic games of football and hurling from the late 1940s until 1990 when the Warwickshire GAA opened its own purpose-built grounds at Pairc na h'Eireann.

The year after this photo was taken Father Murphy's made hurling history when, as an all-Wexford team, they won the Warwickshire Senior Hurling title at Glebe Farm. That remarkable team was captained by Paddy Rochford and included: Eddie O'Brien, Hughie McEvoy, Enda Cummins, Mark Colfer, Jim Mullins, J.J. O'Connor, Aiden O'Neill, John O'Connor, Patsy Morris, Gerry Leary, Matt Doyle, 'Blonde' Goggin, Paddy Eames, Nicky Jackman, John Roche, Pat Cullen, Liam O'Brien and John Fitzgerald.

Another famous day at Glebe Farm came in 1968 when a large crowd watched the Warwickshire GAA footballers defeat Kerry at Glebe Farm.

Cleaning the pool at Fox Hollies Park in the 1960s. The 41-acre park was transferred by the Estates Department between 1929 and 1933. It is cut through by Westley Brook, on which once stood Broomhall Mill.

– and it paid £1,000 towards the cost of the laying out. This was supplemented by £300 from the Birmingham Civic Society. In 1936 the City purchased 25 acres nearby on the Pershore Road South. The cost was £6,500, towards which the Trident Trust gave £2,000 and the Birmingham Playing Fields Association £1,000. This site was now named the Kings Norton Playing Fields whilst the area on the Redditch Road was renamed Kings Norton Park.

Meanwhile on the north of the City, in 1928 the Corporation paid £31,760 for Perry Hall and its 159-acre estate in Perry Barr for the purpose of playing fields. It was helped by £5,000 from Sir Charles Hyde, the owner of the Birmingham Post and Mail; £4,000 from the Feeney Trust; and £3,000 from the National Playing Fields Association.

Significantly the Council itself made a major contribution to the provision of playing fields. As the building of municipal houses accelerated, so too did the transfer of land to the Parks Committee from those committees involved in housing development. Principally these were the Estates Committee, Housing Committee and Public Works. This process began as early as 1920 with the 90 acres of Staple Hall Farm in Northfield and ended on a large-scale in 1935 with the 31.5 acres of the Kettlehouse Estate in Kingstanding.

Sailing on Edgbaston Reservoir in the 1970s, with the Waterworks Tower in the background. Nearby is Perrot's Folly and together they are believed to be the inspiration for 'The Towers' in 'The Lord of the Rings' as Tolkien lived close to here before he went to Oxford University. The reservoir was built as a feeder for the Birmingham Canal.

During that period over 550 acres of land were given over to playing fields or recreation grounds rather than for building upon. This meant that by the end of 1934, Birmingham was providing its citizens with 415 tennis courts (352 grass and 63 hard); 180 football pitches; 115 cricket pitches; 45 bowling greens; seventeen putting greens; and twelve hockey grounds. This was a remarkable achievement.

However, there had been one major problem to resolve with regards to playing fields – whether or not games should be allowed on a Sunday. In 1920 the Parks Committee recommended that tennis and bowls could be played on that day as they would not inconvenience the public and because boating and fishing already took place in some parks. This provoked a controversy in a City that was to continue to restrict activities on a Sunday until the 1970s, in particular with the early closing of public houses.

In 1920, the proposal led to memorials of objection sent to the Council with the result that it rejected the recommendation. Instead by 58 votes to 28 it adopted an amendment that it was 'not satisfied that any public desire has been show for the playing of organised games on a Sunday'. In the absence of any pronounced mandate from ratepayers the Council was 'not prepared to alter the existing practice'.

The matter was later raised again without success but in 1930 the Council resolved to give authority to the Parks Committee to provide facilities for the playing of tennis, bowls and putting in various parks and recreation grounds from 2.00 p.m. until closing time on a Sunday. This change in attitude was affected by the fact that such games were allowed on Sundays in public parks in London and other cities. Small Heath Park and Cannon Hill Park were excepted because of the conditions in the deeds of gift from Louisa Anne Ryland. These had stipulated that 'neither games, boating, nor music should be played on Sundays'.

Footballers at Billesley Common in the 1970s. This extensive area of 91 acres was transferred by the Estates Committee in 1930 as playing fields – at a price to be paid by the Parks Committee that would be determined by a valuer.

Chapter 12

Brighter Birmingham: Parks in War-Time

Birmingham was the second most heavily bombed city in the country during the Second World War, and along with the whole of Merseyside it lost more of its citizens to enemy action than any other place outside London. The Blitz killed 2,241 Brummies and seriously injured another 3,010, with 3,682 harmed slightly. The Luftwaffe's air raids began on 9 August 1940 and ended on 23 April 1943, although the most destructive air

An Air Raid Precautions demonstration at Calthorpe Park on March 3, 1940. Interestingly from its earliest days and because much of it was level, the Park was an exercising ground for the Rifle Volunteers, which later became part of the Territorial Army. For a few years, two guns captured from the Russians during the Crimean War were placed in the Park, but were then returned to the War Department.

An anti-aircraft unit in a Birmingham park.

raids occurred between the end of August 1940 and May 1941. Prolonged and powerful attacks destroyed 12,391 houses, 302 factories, 34 churches, halls and cinemas, and 205 other buildings. Thousands of other properties were damaged.

This Blitz was because of Birmingham's vital importance to the production of munitions. By the end of the war, the workers of the Spitfire factory in Castle Bromwich, were producing 320 Spitfires and 20 Lancasters a month – more aircraft than any other factory in the UK. Elsewhere in the city, at the Longbridge shadow factory, men and women turned out 2,866 Fairey Battles, Hurricanes, Stirlings and Lancasters; whilst at the nearby Austin works almost 500 army and other vehicles were made each week – as well as a multitude of other goods.

The array of war work in Birmingham was staggering. Bristol Hercules engines made at Rover; Lancaster wings, shell cases and bombs manufactured at Fisher and Ludlow's; Spitfire wing spans and light alloy tubing at Reynold's; and plastic components at the GEC. Up to the Battle of Britain all the aero-carburettors for the RAF's Spitfires and Hurricanes were made at SU Carburettors – and if it had been destroyed the air force would have suffered a mortal blow. Serck produced all the radiators and air coolers for these planes.

Workers at the Dunlop, Kynoch's, the Norton, James Cycle, Lucas, the Metropolitan-Cammell, Morris Commercial, the Wolseley, and the BSA (Birmingham Small Arms) all strove hard for victory. Indeed, when the BSA was hit badly in November 1940, Churchill himself was alarmed at the consequent national fall in the making of rifles.

Smaller firms were also crucial. Turner Brothers made a wide range of jigs and tools critical for aircraft production; Eddystone Radio and the Monitor Radio Company were significant in their field; jewellers turned their hands to intricate parts; and Hudson's Whistles supplied whistles to the Royal Navy and others. By 1944, 400,000 Brummies were involved in war work – a greater percentage of the population than anywhere else in the UK.

The ramifications of total war profoundly affected Birmingham's parks. In 1938, trench shelters were dug in some of them. Most could take 50 people and were reinforced with steel, concrete and linings. A year later, steel air raid shelters supplied by the Home Office became features of parks and recreation grounds in the south-west of the City such as Cotteridge Park, Highgate Park, Kings Heath Park and Selly Park. In addition, large areas of some recreation grounds were ploughed for the growing of food; whilst anti-aircraft units were placed in some parks and others were used for Air Raid Precautions Volunteers (ARP) exercises.

Changes to the physical landscape of parks and recreation grounds were matched by changes in their use. In 1940, and for the first time, all organised games were allowed to be played on a Sunday in Birmingham's parks. Deemed a concession, it was made to allow recreation for war workers; however, so popular was this supposedly war-time measure that it became long-term in 1946 when the Council finally approved the playing of all games during the normal hours of the opening of parks on a Sunday.

A more expansive policy was as obvious with respect to entertainments in parks. In the late 1850s and 1860s, Aston Park had been the venue for large-scale fêtes that drew enormous crowds. After it came under municipal control, there were no such big and organised festivities in the Park until 1906 when it was one of several where celebrations were held for the 70th birthday of Joseph Chamberlain. By contrast most parks' entertainment was smaller-scale and focused on the playing of music by the Police Band, in particular, and the performance of concerts by various bodies.

This continued during the inter-war years and in the summer months of 1936 to 1939, the Police Band played concerts on Wednesdays, Saturdays and Sundays. Bandstands were also used for concert parties and a Punch and Judy show; whilst local bands and choirs were allowed free use of bandstands as long as they made their own arrangements for ticketing and stewarding.

Within a year of the war starting, the concert parties were discontinued, although the City Transport Band and some military bands did put on performances and the Punch and Judy shows were carried on. No programme of entertainment at all was organised by the Parks Committee in 1941, but it did assist the Lord Mayor's War Relief Committee in arranging an innovative and adventurous six-week season of plays. These were presented by Basil Langton's Travelling Repertory Theatre Company in the open at Cannon Hill, Aston, Handsworth and Ward End Parks.

As an actor and director, Langton made an invaluable contribution to the war-time British stage. Classically trained, powerful of voice and manner, he was an idealist who wished to bring new audiences to serious drama by touring outside London. Such beliefs were shared by Sir Barry Jackson, the founder of the Birmingham Repertory Theatre. He was passionate about developing new acting talent and presenting plays that were challenging and ground-breaking.

In 1941 Langton's Travelling Repertory Theatre re-opened the Birmingham Repertory with 'Cricket on the Hearth'. It remained in residence for a year, putting on 20 plays produced by Sir Barry Jackson. The season of these 'Plays in the Park' ended with a full-length version of 'Hamlet' with Langton in the title role and Paul Scofield playing Horatio. Born in Birmingham, Scofield would become noted for his acting talent and for his distinctive voice and delivery; indeed he went on to receive both an Academy Award and a BAFTA Award for his performance as Sir Thomas More in the 1966 film 'A Man for All Seasons'. With Birmingham as his base, for the rest of the war Langton took his company to blitzed towns, munitions factories and Army camps to perform plays by Shakespeare, Shaw, and Euripides, as well as modern drama.

A huge advertisement for 'Plays in the Park' on the side of Birmingham's Town Hall in the Second World War.

Following the success of these 'Plays in the Park', in 1942 the Government asked local authorities to encourage people to spend their holidays at home. In response, the General Purposes Committee of Birmingham Council sanctioned an extensive programme of bands, orchestras, concert parties, variety, dancing and other attractions to be staged in parks in the summer. This became known as 'Brighter Birmingham'. The Lord Mayor's War Relief Fund Committee also presented a nine weeks' season of plays in Cannon Hill, Lightwoods and Handsworth Parks. Again they were in the open but a marquee was kept in reserve for performances in bad weather.

A year later the 'Brighter Birmingham' programme was extended and more than one thousand entertainments were given in the parks; whilst another nine weeks' season of 'Plays in the Park' was held in marquee theatres. From 1944 the city was divided into zones for 'Brighter Birmingham' and voluntary local committees assisted with the arrangements. Events included a horse show at Kings Heath Park; a cycle polo match at the putting green and tennis courts at Queen's Park, Harborne; a dog show at Calthorpe Park; and physical training and dance displays by teachers and children from Birmingham schools. Once again the Travelling Repertory Theatre Company undertook the season of plays for the Lord Mayor's War Relief Fund Committee.

With the coming of peace in 1945 the City Council delegated to the Parks Committee the organisation of the 'Holidays at Home' programme. Entertainments

Dancing at The Dell in Muntz Park in the 1940s.

The Hall of Memory and Civic Centre Gardens in 1972. Thanks to the late Harold Wareham and his son Ken. The Civic Gardens were laid out in the later 1930s and were swept away for the development of Centenary Square. They were one of the venues for 'Brighter Birmingham' entertainments.

were held at marquee theatres in twelve parks; band concerts were staged in the Civic Centre Gardens in Broad Street; and there was open-air dancing at Muntz Park. The Lord Mayor's War Relief Fund Committee again organised the 'Plays in the Park' and engaged a company to present a three-play repertory at Cannon Hill, Lightwoods, Handsworth and Rookery Parks.

These entertainments in the park became annual events and in 1948 they included a short experimental season of plays given for the first time in Great Britain in an arena theatre. From then on all plays were presented this way and in 1950 the Arena Theatre Company presented a repertory of five plays on their horse-shoe shaped stage. The audience was seated on three sides and the whole was enclosed in specially-constructed oval-shaped marquee.

These 'Brighter Birmingham' entertainments also included variety shows, concerts and children's entertainments that were given in nine summer theatres built in large marquees; whilst band concerts continued to be held in the Civic Gardens and open-air dancing at Muntz Park. By the early 1950s support for these events was declining but entertainment in Birmingham's parks was soon to be revived in spectacular fashion by a powerful politician from the back streets who was motivated by opening up the arts to his own people: he was Sir Frank Price.

Chapter 13

Parks, Art and Tulip Festivals

Frank Price came from the back streets of Hockley and he never forgot where he came from or the loyalty that he owed to his own people. Elected to the Council in 1949, he would become one of the most important figures in post-war Birmingham and was knighted in 1966 when he was Lord Mayor. For all this honour and others, he remained true to his roots. As a politician Sir Frank was determined to improve life for the working-class of the city – not only through redevelopment but also through provisions for culture and leisure.

A dynamic and forceful chairman of the powerful Public Works Committee from 1953-59, he played a pivotal role in a massive programme of building new

Alderman Frank Price, with the binoculars, at one of Birmingham's Tulip Festivals in Cannon Hill Park.

A matinee performance of 'The Taming of the Shrew' in the arena of Cannon Hill Park in the summer of 1953. Plays such as this followed on from the wartime entertainments organised by the 'Brighter Birmingham' scheme.

homes and of a radical road scheme later known as the Inner Ring Road. It is less well known that he pushed for the creation of an arts centre for local children and young people. To this end he invited John English, a playwright and theatre director, and his wife Alicia (Mollie) Randle to join him.

As Sir Frank recalled in his memoir *'Being There'* (2002) 'the Parks Department did sterling work during the war years, helping to keep up the spirits of those working long hours on sparse rations and not much to smile about, by creating what were called 'Holidays at Home''. Amongst the events that were laid on were 'Plays in the Park', whereby John English and Molly Randle 'worked tirelessly to bring some fun and a little culture into the lives of people who, at the time, had a little of either'. The plays were held in a large marquee for 'theatre in the round'. Most of the actors were professionals and in some children participated. These shows were subsidised by the Council and were so successful that they continued long after the end of war.

Whilst he was still chairman of the Public Works Committee, Sir Frank was deeply concerned that the arts was the preserve of the wealthy and that 'many of the middle-class thought subsidising the arts an unacceptable burden, which meant that the poor had no chance to share in the pleasures the arts brought'. In particular he was resolved to ensure that working-class children were not 'cultural orphans'. He wanted a place where young people from five to 25 could watch, listen and participate in a wide range of artistic activities. With John English and Molly Randle he did something about it and in 1964 the Midlands Arts Centre for Children and Young People, now the MAC, opened.

Sir Frank also had a passion for parks and for their importance as places of leisure and culture and in 1959 he became chairman of the Parks Committee. With the drive and enthusiasm that marked all that he did, he revived entertainments in the city's parks and made Cannon Hill Park a focal point. Most notably he introduced fireworks displays, jazz festivals and the Tulip Festival. This latter event came about after he had heard that the Dutch were organising a 'Floriade' to celebrate the 400th anniversary of the introduction of tulips from Turkey. It prompted the 'idea of brightening up the city after what proved to be a long, cold, dull winter' by holding a Tulip Festival in the spring of 1960.

Acting on his own initiative during the summer recess of the Council and certain that the event would make a profit, Sir Frank instructed the general manager of the Parks Department to order £9,000 worth of tulip bulbs. It was a considerable sum but Sir Frank wanted 'enough to flood a park and the public flower beds around the city'. He then flew to the Netherlands to meet representatives of the Dutch Tourist and Trade Departments to see if he could obtain any help from them.

He succeeded and amongst other things they promised to set up a mock Dutch village with a windmill in the park; gift 1,000 tulip bulbs; and send over a clog maker, lace maker and 24 young women who would hand out fresh tulips that would be flown into Birmingham every other day on a scheduled flight. During this trip, Sir Frank was also introduced to the Boesmans, who were well-known balloonists. For a fee of £400 they agreed to bring over their balloon.

Upon his return, there was a furore over what Sir Frank had done, but with the support of Alderman Annie Wood, the leader of the Conservatives on the Parks Committee, he defeated his own colleagues who had wanted to censure him. Next, Sir Frank enlisted the support of Sir Eric Clayson, the managing director of the Birmingham Post and Mail, who agreed to cover the event with editorial and to arrange a photographic competition. Sir Eric also offered £600 for the advert that was to be wrapped around the Boesmans' balloon.

The Tulip Festival was planned for April 30 to May 14, 1960 in Cannon Hill Park – but with just weeks to go there was a severe cold spell. The park's gardeners feared that the quarter of a million tulip bulbs would not flower in time but Sir Frank 'had the workshop make semi-triangular shades under which we placed electric strip lights'. These not only helped the bulbs to flower in time but 'added to the attraction as dusk fell over the park, illuminating the flower beds'.

Part of the Dutch village at a Tulip Festival.

Young Dutch women at a Tulip Festival.

The Tulip Express by the 'Golden Lion'.

Members of the Parks Committee on their annual inspection of Cannon Hill Park in August 20, 1954. Thanks to Del Wilford, nee Jones.

The Lady Mayoress, Mrs. O. Jones, and the Lord Mayor, Joseph Balmer, inspecting the green houses at Cannon Hill Park on August 20, 1954. Thanks to Del Wilford, nee Jones.

Then on the Thursday before the opening 'we enjoyed the hottest spring weather for years'. Sir Frank's luck held. The previous October the decision had been made to erect an open-air theatre and book professional artists to entertain the crowds until 10.00 pm, when there would be a fireworks display. One of those artists was 'a little-known song and dance man by the name of Roy Castle'. A few months after he was booked, he appeared on American television and earned rave reviews. He became a huge star and his fees rose massively but to his credit Roy Castle honoured his booking with Birmingham at 'a paltry fee'.

In another piece of good fortune, Max Bygraves was appearing at the Coventry Hippodrome. He had made 'Tulips from Amsterdam' a hit song and so Sir Frank rang him 'to ask if he would open our Festival and he agreed to do it'. He made a sensational appearance that was matched on the afternoon of the last day of the Festival by the Boesmans. As their balloon rose for the last time the band played 'Now is the hour, when we must say goodbye'. Sir Frank found 'it difficult to

The Cannon Hill Park Restaurant in the 1950s.

A wonderful photograph from the late 1950s of West Indian men chatting; it was taken by the late Edwin Millington.

describe the wave of emotion that swept through the crowd'. Some sang, others wept as if they were saying goodbye to friends.

The Tulip Festival was a huge success. It had resonances with the Fête Champêtres held at Aston Hall back in 1856 and with the event at which Blondin had appeared in 1861. And as for Sir Frank Price, in his belief that working-class men, women and children should have access to arts and culture then he was a worthy successor to the likes of John Alfred Langford, Daniel O'Neill and other working men who had fought so staunchly for the provision of public parks in Birmingham.

Over 500,000 people had paid to visit the Tulip Festival. The profits from it funded the provision of hot showers near to the football and rugby pitches in city parks. The Tulip Festival continued to be a big success for a number of years. Sir Frank organised three more and ran water festivals, military tattoos and used the open-air theatre at Cannon Hill Park for concerts by the bands of Ted Heath and Humphrey Lyttleton.

Feeding the ducks in the 1960s.

An aerial view of the fairground in 1970.

Asian dancers in the 1970s.

He also 'started the first Guy Fawkes Bonfire Night festivals for these kids who lived in flats on housing estates and who would miss the thrill of watching a bonfire or organised firework displays'. The idea had originally been that of Councillor Mrs Johnson but previous chairmen of the Parks Committee had dismissed her suggestions as nonsense. Sir Frank was very pleased for her that they turned out to be so successful and a date in the city's annual calendar of outdoor events.

Over The Rec: An Afterword

As kids we were always 'going over the rec' after school in the light nights or else all day in the summer holidays. Our rec was Sarehole Mill Recreation Ground and we used to explore the island that lay between two forks of the River Cole; jump across the narrower of the forks from one bank to another; swing from a piece of thick rope tied to a tree over the wider fork; make snowmen in the winter; and often just mooch about.

And always looming large in the background was the empty and decaying Sarehole Mill. We were unaware then of its connections with Tolkien, who had lived just across the way in a house in Wake Green Road that was then part of the hamlet of Sarehole. Years later, though, we found out that the look of Gandalf the white wizard in *'The Hobbit'* and *'The Lord of the Rings'* had been inspired by the millers, the Andrews brothers who were always covered in flour.

Fortunately the Mill and its water meadow had been left to the City by its owner A. H. Foster to be kept in perpetuity as an open space for the benefit of the public. The meadow was turned into 'our rec', Sarehole Mill, but the Mill itself was going to be knocked down by the Council. This roused local people to campaign for its restoration. In a rare victory in the 1960s, they won and in 1969 Sarehole Mill was opened to the public as a City Museum.

Sometimes we would go beyond 'our rec' and the Mill and walk through what we knew as Cole Bank with its football fields. Aged about ten I had played my first game of proper football there for Moseley Church of England School against Christchurch, Sparkbrook; we had lost. We also played on the sloping pitch at the Dell, just off the Yardley Wood Road. I can still feel my chest heaving as I tried to catch my breath as I chased a heavy, sodden case ball uphill – only to have to turn round and run back panting as it was hoofed down the pitch. The Dell is now Joy's Wood, named in memory of Joy Fifer who played such a pivotal role in saving from development Moseley Bog, another inspirational place for Tolkien.

Anyway once we reached Cole Bank we would string out precariously along the river bank. This is now part of the Millstream Way and is called the John Morris Jones Way, commemorating a teacher, geographer, historian and researcher who was one of the key figures in laying the foundations for local history and local geography in Birmingham. However, when we were kids there was no clear way, we had to push through foliage and branches till we got to Brook Lane.

Across the road was an old bridge over the River Cole and this led into the mysterious area called The Dingles. Long and narrow, it stretched all the way along the Cole Valley Road almost to Trittiford Mill Park with its huge pool and the Chinn Brook Recreation Ground. Me and our Kid, Darryl, always felt a sense of ownership to this last place. This was because of a story passed down in the family that the stream itself was named after our great, great grandfather Henry Chinn – the one who had been a tenant farmer in Kings Heath and then the bailiff on the Cartland Estate before he had died in an accident. We cannot do so now as I have found out since that the name Chinn Brook predates my family by hundreds of years.

With its gnarled trees, tangled hedgerows, big island and expanses of grassland, The Dingles was beyond our own territory. Nearer to home and just across from Sarehole Rec was a more impenetrable place. It ran from Green Road along the Cole to the bridge at Springfield. When we were young it had a narrow path, hemmed in by the river to one side and on the other by a mass of old trees and saplings mingled with rampant shrubs that were mostly set in boggy ground.

About three parts of the way down it got even denser until the allotments. If you were feeling adventurous you could carry on and tentatively follow the banks of the river to the bridge, just before which the water cascaded down what we called

Formal gardens at Cole Bank Playing Fields in the 1950s. I don't remember these in the late 1960s, only football fields. Originally this area had been Cotterill's Meadow.

rapids. Of course they were no such thing but even though the Cole was a little river, when it rained heavily it flooded quickly and the water would pelt down especially fast down this spot.

I have a recollection that sometimes we called this wild land 'the Teddy Bear Fields' for an unknown reason. Much of the wildness was soon to disappear when a riverside walk was constructed in about 1969. A Charles Hougham had given this stretch for a waterside promenade as far back as 1913, so it had taken a few decades for his aims to be fulfilled. Now part of the Millstream Way, the walk has really opened up the Cole Valley and that has been a boon, but with its coming went a lot of the fascination of a secret and enchanting place.

As we grew older, playing football over the rec became more and more important. We'd play shots in if there were only a few of us, or have kickabouts if there were enough of us. Goal posts were made with jumpers and sweaters and as soon as a game got started other kids would always come across and ask 'can we have a game'. Soon there could be 20 or more aside. In the dinner hour during the summer holidays though, we always had to give way to the blue-overalled young men from Perry Brothers, the motor windscreen makers down Sarehole Road.

As we got older our games became more organised, especially on a Sunday afternoon when Our Dad, Buck Chinn, would come with us. A few other men like him would join us and the ages would range from early teens to blokes in their 40s. But it was dad who was like a pied piper, pulling us altogether, organising us into sides and calming things down when things occasionally got a bit heated.

If we were early enough we would usually go over to Cole Bank where there were proper goal posts. We had games lasting two or three hours and there were some fine footballers, including my mate Dave Evans and Noel Fagan, who went on to play for the Villa. Those kickabouts led us to form a proper team, Sarehole Saracens. We were in the Selly Oak League and played on many sports grounds across the city. Glebe Farm was one that always stood out because of the games of Irish Football, and my eyes were often drawn from our pitch to watch the handling and kicking of a captivating game.

Parks, recreation grounds and playing fields were vital aspects of my upbringing. Our Dad always talked about playing in the Little Park on the Ladypool Road; whilst Our Mom would tell us about spending her school holidays in Aston Park, or else at Salford Park. When we were little Mom and Dad would take us with Nan and Grandad Perry to Cannon Hill Park. Granddad was in a wheelchair as he could not walk because of multiple sclerosis and we always played close to him.

Our Dad would park in Russell Road and we would plant ourselves in the corner by Edgbaston Road and close to the glass houses that so fascinated us. After a while we'd have a walk around and we would always be drawn to the big boulder by the boating lake. We had notions that it was a meteorite that had come down from space,

I met my wife, Kay, in Benidorm on two occasions in the summer of 1977. She was from Dublin and came to Birmingham on a Sunday early in January 1978. That was the third time we had met and we became engaged. On the Sunday afternoon we went over the rec to Sarehole Mill. As you can see it was covered in snow – and no, I didn't actually throw her off the bridge!

particularly when 'Superman' was all the rage; but it seems that it was a boulder left over from the passing of a glacier in the Ice Age. Then as we reached twelve or thirteen we would go each year with our mates to the Tulip Festival. I have vivid memories of the tulips, of course, but also of Dutch chocolate, windmills, Dutch women in national dress, and the fair.

Like all Brummies of my generation, I was brought up to be proud of Birmingham as an active municipality. Our Mom and Dad always emphasised that we drank the softest and most beautiful water in the world from Wales because the City built the Elan Valley dams and reservoirs; we were proud to have our own police force until 1974 when I was seventeen; and my first bank account was with the Birmingham Municipal Bank.

We Brummies also knew that the Council had been essential in providing parks, as had benefactors. What we did not know is that there was a third group responsible for providing free parks for the people. That was the working men of the 1850s and

60s who campaigned, organised, raised funds and battled for the rights of working-class men, women and children to enjoy public parks and recreation grounds. I was raised in a class conscious family and yet we knew nothing of the efforts of these determined and motivated men; nor, I suspect, did any other Brummies. These men had either been excluded from the histories of the City and the Council or else mentioned briefly. Thus they and their valiant efforts were forgotten. No more.

Birmingham's parks are a gift that has been passed on to us thanks to the efforts of four distinct groups. The first comprises generous upper-class and upper middle-class philanthropists of a variety of backgrounds and beliefs. The second embraces preachers like George Dawson and Robert Dale, who propounded the Civic Gospel. The third is the Council. In its early years and with a few honourable exceptions like Alderman Cutler, it was dominated by councillors with a miserable attitude to civic life. Thankfully they were eventually replaced by dynamic councillors who enthusiastically took up the Civic Gospel so as to provide municipal facilities for its people. The fourth group was a hardy and resourceful band of working-class activists who were resolved to improve life for their fellows. Together these groups succeeded in providing free parks for the people. They have left us a wonderful legacy that we should cherish.